Affordable Family Fun!

by
Susan L. Lingo

Loveland, Colorado

Dedication

With love to my two favorite playmates, Dane and Lindsay.
I'll never forget the parking lot sculptures
in Grand Island!

AFFORDABLE FAMILY FUN
Copyright © 1998 Susan L. Lingo

Credits
Editor: Bob Buller
Chief Creative Officer: Joani Schultz
Copy Editor: Janis Sampson
Designer and Art Director: Jean Bruns
Cover Art Director: Jeff A. Storm
Computer Graphic Artist: Joyce Douglas
Cover Designer and Illustrator: Ken Bowser
Illustrators: Ken Bowser and Jan Knudson
Production Manager: Gingar Kunkel

Library of Congress Cataloging-in-Publication Data
Lingo, Susan L.
   Affordable family fun / by Susan L. Lingo.
      p.   cm.
   Includes index.
   ISBN 0-7644-2032-1 (alk. paper)
   1. Family--Religious life. 2. Family--Prayer-books and devotions--English. I. Title.
BV4526.2.L56   1997
249--dc21   97-40097
                                                                              CIP

10 9 8 7 6 5 4 3 2 1   07 06 05 04 03 02 01 00 99 98
Printed in the United States of America.

Contents

Family Field Trips

places to Go & Things to Do

Homespun Fun
Things to Do & Make at Home

Family Festivals

Pleasin' Parties, Festive Foods
& Holiday Celebrations

Introduction

WHERE CAN WE GO? WHAT CAN WE DO?
EVERYTHING COSTS TOO MUCH!

What can a family do together on a shoestring budget? Plenty! In *Affordable Family Fun* you'll find oodles of exciting family-focused ideas for great together-times. It's important for families to play together, but when can they learn about God at the same time, the impact is incredible! In today's world of instant entertainment, fix-me-quick meals, and a "hurry, we're late" mentality, it's more crucial than ever for families to purposefully set aside quality time to spend together. Quality time. Purposefully. These are key values in creating meaningful family relationships.

The activities and ideas in this book are designed to be real "budget buddies" for families. Every idea can be enjoyed for under five dollars, and many involve no cost at all. So you have no excuse to avoid family activities and every reason to spend time together.

WHAT DO FAMILIES GET WHEN THEY SPEND TIME TOGETHER?

● **Families get closer.** Families who spend quality time together have substantially fewer problems communicating, spend less time dealing with behavior issues, and develop more empathy toward each other.

• **Families get talking.** We all know that practice makes perfect, and this is just as true for family communications as for anything else. Too often family members speak in quick, one-word sentences or simply ignore each other's thoughts and feelings altogether. Sadly, young children often pay the greatest price with this. Busy parents and older siblings tend to brush aside young children and create walls of hurt and misunderstanding. But spending time together allows every family member to talk about and share his or her feelings, thoughts, hopes, and dreams.

• **Families get happy!** Look at families who spend quality time together, and you'll see lots of smiles. Guaranteed! Nothing beats the bond of shared experiences and fun that are created when a family enjoys time together. And don't forget to include grandparents. Age and happiness are not mutually exclusive, so sharing family fun with grandparents is equally enriching for the youngest and for the oldest family members.

WHAT MAKES THIS BOOK AN EXCITING FAMILY RESOURCE?

Affordable Family Fun is divided into three sections: Family Field Trips, which includes unique places to visit and sights to share; Homespun Fun, which is packed full of great things to make and do at home; and Family Festivals, which contains twelve incredible ideas for fantastic parties and impromptu celebrations—one for each month of the year! Over forty memorable fun-times that also teach important biblical truths. Where else can you find such outstanding fun and God-centered learning?

So what are you waiting for? Grab the family, hold onto your hats, and dive into the following pages for some good ol' fashioned family fun!

Family Field Trips

places to Go & Things to Do

Rings in the Water

Families will learn that when they tell others about
God's love, that love spreads far and wide.

BIBLE CONCEPT:
We can tell others about God's love.

SCRIPTURE BASIS:
Matthew 28:19-20

SUPPLIES:
You'll need paper bags, grapes, sandwiches, juice,
paper cups, and napkins.

PREPARATION:
Prepare a simple picnic lunch of grape "pebbles," chilled juice, and
sandwich "stones." Use a cookie cutter or the rim of a drinking glass
to cut the sandwiches into circular shapes. Then decide on a good
place to gather small stones, rocks, and pebbles—such as along a
gravel road or stream bed. You'll also need to select a small pond or
lake to visit.

Fun is just a "stone's throw" away in this simple activity that
adults love as much as children.

Hand each child a paper bag as you say: **Let's gather stones
and pebbles in these bags and go on a fun adventure. We'll toss
our stones into water and watch what happens to the water.**

10

Then we'll enjoy a special picnic lunch together.

After you've collected bags full of small stones and pebbles, drive, walk, or bike to the pond or lake you've chosen as your picnic spot. Encourage children to toss their stones into the water and watch the spreading rings. Point out how nice the splashes sound and ask young children whether big or little stones make the largest splashes. Keep young hearts and minds focused on God by making comments such as "Isn't it great that God gave us ears to hear water splashing?" and "I'm glad God gave us beautiful lakes and rivers to enjoy."

Try tossing a handful of pebbles into the water at one time, then a single stone. Which make larger rings in the water? How do the rings spread? Invite children to toss one stone close to shore and one as far out into the lake as they can throw. How do the rings in the water compare?

After the bags are half empty, gather children for a special picnic lunch of grape "pebbles," sandwich "stones," and cool juice. As you enjoy your treats, hold up a stone and ask: **What will happen if I toss this stone into the water?** Pause for responses. Then say: **This one little stone makes lots of rings in the water. The rings start out small but keep getting larger and wider, don't they? This is how it is when we tell others about God's love. When we tell one person about God's love, that person tells another person and then another—and soon God's love spreads everywhere! The Bible tells us that we can tell people close to home or far away— just as we tossed stones near the shore and far out into the lake. The news about God's love will spread far and wide** wherever **we tell others about him. Isn't that wonderful?**

Help children focus their faith by asking:

- **Who can you tell about God this week?**
- **What can you tell that person about God?**

When your picnic is finished, invite children to toss the rest of their stones into the water. Encourage children to call out the name of a person they can tell about God each time a stone is tossed. Then have children keep one stone as a reminder to tell others about God's love. (If your child is three or younger, make sure the stone is larger than a fifty cent piece to avoid choking dangers.)

Use the empty grocery sacks as litter bags as you clean up your picnic area.

Sticky Squares

family ♥ goal:

Families will realize that God gives us beautiful gifts in nature because he loves us.

BIBLE CONCEPT:
God created all of nature.

SCRIPTURE BASIS:
Genesis 1:1–2:4a

SUPPLIES:
You'll need scissors, tape or safety pins, and a roll of clear self-adhesive paper.

PREPARATION:
Cut the clear self-adhesive paper into twelve-inch squares, one for each person. Leave the backing on the self-adhesive paper. Then decide where you will take your nature walk. Consider places such as the woods, a nature trail, the park, or even your own yard.

What's more fun than a walk in the park? Taking the park "home" with you!

Just before your walk, peel the backing from the self-adhesive paper squares. Carefully tape or pin the self-adhesive paper to the front of each person's shirt so the sticky side is facing out.

Say: **We know that God made the world and all the beautiful things we see in nature. Let's see how many different things we can find. When you find a weed or flower or twig or leaf that you especially like, stick it to the paper on your tummy. Let's see if we can fill our sticky squares with things God made.**

As you take a leisurely walk, point out that even though God made all the leaves, each one is different and special, just like people. Explain that God is the only Creator and that he made the world beautiful for us to enjoy and care for. Encourage family members to stick many kinds, colors, and sizes of grasses, leaves, and flowers to their sticky squares.

When your sticky squares are filled, ask your family to point out their favorite items and explain why those items are special. Ask questions such as "Why do you think God made so many things in nature?" and "How can we care for the beautiful world God has given us?"

Say: **God created the world for us to enjoy. God made the world beautiful because he loves us. So let's remember to thank God every day for the wonderful gifts of flowers and trees and bushes and grass that he has given us.**

After your walk, carefully remove the sticky squares. You may want to glue or tape the squares to poster board, then encourage family members to hang these "natural" posters in their rooms to remind them to thank God for his gifts of nature. Older children may enjoy using a nature book or encyclopedia to identify the types of plants or trees from which their natural treasures came.

terrific tip
You may wish to cover the sticky squares with another sheet of self-adhesive paper to make unusual place mats, greeting cards, or framed pictures.

Fantastic French Fry Contest

family ♥ goal:

Family members will learn that each person in the family has God-given talents that can be used to honor God.

BIBLE CONCEPT:
God has given each of us special gifts.

SCRIPTURE BASIS:
1 Corinthians 12:4-11

SUPPLIES:
You'll need scissors, yellow construction paper, tape, a black marker, and three eight-inch pieces of blue ribbon.

PREPARATION:
Choose to visit three restaurants that serve french fries. Consider small cafes, fast-food restaurants, and steak houses.

Everyone in the family will enjoy this taste-tempting together time.

Before the french fry contest, set out yellow construction paper, scissors, tape, a black marker, and the blue ribbons.

Say: **Today we're going to have a french fry contest to determine who has the best french fries. French fries may all look similar, but each has it's own "gifts." Some fries may be hotter than others. Some may have just the right amount of salt. And some may be made from the whitest potatoes. So let's make blue ribbons and award them to the best of the best french fries!**

Have family members work together to create three blue ribbon french fry awards. Cut heart, circle, or star shapes from the yellow construction paper, then write the name of the award on each shape.

Use categories such as "Hottest Fries," "Best Tasting Fries," or "Crispiest Fries." Finally, tape a blue ribbon to each award.

Visit each restaurant you've chosen and taste the fries, but don't hand out the awards yet! At the last restaurant, decide which blue ribbons should be awarded to which restaurants. Then retrace your steps as you present your awards to the managers of each food establishment.

When you're homeward bound, say: **We know that God created each of us. But did you know that God created each of us in a special way? Even though we may all look similar, God has given each one of us special gifts. Just as the french fries have different "gifts," God gave each person different gifts, talents, and abilities. Some of us are great at painting. Some of us are better at math. And some of us are super at singing songs or writing book reports. We all have different gifts because God made each of us unique. And we can use those talents and gifts to show God how much we love him. We can pray for others, help them with work, or even sing songs to someone who's not feeling well. It's important to identify and use the different gifts God has given us.**

Then spend some time visiting about the God-gifts each person in your family has been given. Help each other identify the gifts God has given you. Then ask family members to explain ways they can share their gifts with others. Point out that when you use those gifts to help people, it's like you're giving them an award of love from God.

Catch a Wondrous Web

Families will discover the importance of trusting in God's strength to make them strong.

BIBLE CONCEPT:
Our trust in God is strongest when we love him most.

SCRIPTURE BASIS:
Job 8:13-15

SUPPLIES:
You'll need a can of hair spray and black or dark blue construction paper.

PREPARATION:
Choose a place outdoors where you've observed spider's webs. Webs can generally be found along low bushes and shrubs, tall grass and weeds, or trailing from houses and other buildings.

This unusual family activity works best on a dewy summer morning.

Hand each family member several sheets of black or dark blue construction paper. Explain that you'll be going on a "spider's web safari" to collect webs on your papers. Take a walk around the area you've chosen to explore. When someone spots a spider's web, carefully hold the construction paper against the back of the web. Then spray the entire spider's web with hair spray. The sticky mist should transfer the web to the paper. Use a new sheet of paper each time you discover a new spider's web.

When you've collected all the webs you can find, examine the fine threads of the web. Then have family members discuss the following questions. Ask:

16

- What does the spider's web remind you of?
- Does the web seem strong or fragile? Explain.
- What do you think happens to a spider's web in a strong wind or when something brushes against it?
- The Bible tells us that people who don't love God are fragile. Why do you think this is true?
- How do you think we can develop a stronger trust in God?

Say: **Because a spider's web is thin and fragile, it breaks apart very easily. We need more than the strength of a spider's web, so it's important to trust God in all we do. Trust is made strong by love, so when we love and follow God, our trust in him grows even stronger. Let's hang our spider web "pictures" on the wall so we can remember that only love for God can make our trust in him strong and unbreakable.**

terrific tip Older children might enjoy re-spraying their webs with hair spray or other spray adhesive, then carefully sprinkling the webs with shimmery glitter. Hang the wondrous webs in a place for everyone to enjoy.

The Dollar Game

family ♥ goal:

Families will recognize the importance of being kind and thoughtful to those around them.

BIBLE CONCEPT:

God wants us to share with and do nice things for others.

SCRIPTURE BASIS:

Acts 20:35b

SUPPLIES:

You'll need a Bible, wrapping paper, tape, and one dollar for each family member. (You may need a few cents extra for tax.)

PREPARATION:

Choose a store where you'll be able to purchase small items for one dollar or less. Consider close-out stores, discount houses, dollar shops, and discount drugstores.

This contagious game will delight the entire family with gifts and giggles.

After you arrive at the store you've chosen to visit, decide who will buy a gift for whom. Then hand each family member one dollar (plus tax on one dollar, if necessary). Say: **We each have one dollar to spend on a surprise gift for someone in the family. Your job is to find the neatest or prettiest or best surprise gift in the store for that dollar. It might be something useful or something just for fun. We'll meet in the front of the store in twenty minutes. Ready? Go!**

terrific tip

You may wish to designate a category for shopping such as finding the silliest gift, the most useful gift, an edible gift, the tiniest gift, or the most gifts for one dollar.

Have young children accompany adults and secretly pick out their favorite gifts. Assure young children that you won't peek as you help them pay for the items. When everyone is gathered at the front of the store, return home to gift wrap your surprise treasures. To add excitement and anticipation, tell family members you'll open your gifts after dinner.

When you're ready to open the surprise gifts, read aloud the last half of Acts 20:35. Open the gifts, then ask family members the following questions:

- **Did you have fun choosing a gift for someone? Explain.**
- **How did you feel as you opened your surprise gift?**
- **Was it more fun to give a gift or to receive a gift? Why?**
- **How do you think others felt when they received their gifts?**
- **What gifts that don't cost anything can we give to each other?**

Let each family member reveal who bought each gift and why it was chosen. Encourage family members to thank one another for their thoughtfulness and creativity in gift giving.

terrific tip

Older children enjoy spontaneity in this great activity. Have a mini-celebration by going out for an inexpensive treat such as french fries and soft drinks, and then opening the gifts in the restaurant.

No Junk Allowed!

Families will understand that each family member has God-given value and is a reason for celebration.

BIBLE CONCEPT:
Each of us is valuable in God's sight.

SCRIPTURE BASIS:
Genesis 1:27

SUPPLIES:
You'll need colorful markers and paper grocery bags.

PREPARATION:
Map out a route for a walk.

I n this unusual scavenger hunt, family members learn that "God don't make no junk!"

Have family members form pairs (or trios), then hand each pair a paper grocery bag. Invite pairs to decorate their bags with colorful markers. Have pairs choose one partner to be the "bag-carrier" and one (or two) to be "picker-uppers."

Then say: **When we say that something has value, we mean that it's worth a lot, that it's not junk. Let's play an unusual game to learn about what's valuable. As we take a walk, be on the lookout for junk such as bottle caps, papers, nuts, bolts, squashed cans, and anything else you may see. When you or your partner find a piece of junk, the picker-upper in your pair is to pick it up and hold it as you look for another piece of junk. Then, when you find another piece of junk, you and your partner must decide which is more valuable: the piece of junk you're holding or the piece you just found. Hold the piece you think is most valuable and put the other piece of junk in your bag. When we get home, we'll examine our "valuables."**

As you walk along, point out that each piece of junk collected was created for some special use. Explain that junk isn't created to be junk—it only turns out that way if it's neglected and forgotten. After your walk, return home and examine the items each pair has collected. Then discuss the following questions:

- **Why did you pick up the pieces that you did?**
- **For what useful purpose was each item made?**
- **Can junk be cleaned up so it's no longer junk? How?**
- **Do you ever feel as though you are "junk"? Explain.**

Say: **We all feel worthless or not valued at times—like pieces of junk. Maybe we get poor grades on tests, or we feel as though nobody notices the good things we do. But God created us in his image, and God didn't make junk! God made us and loves us, so we have value. Value to help others, value to learn about God, and value to love ourselves. When we begin to feel "junky," we get rusty at loving God, other people, and ourselves. But when we remember that God values us, we are able to clean away the rust and shine his love to those around us.**

Now choose one piece of junk from your collection, and set it in your room to remind you that God doesn't make junk!

Sheep Safari

family ♥ goal:

Families will learn that God always wants us close to him, so he looks for us when we become lost.

BIBLE CONCEPT:
God searches for us when we're lost from him.

SCRIPTURE BASIS:
Luke 15:4-7

SUPPLIES:
You'll need a Bible, tape, scissors, a bag of large marshmallows, and photocopies of the "Sheep" pattern from page 23.

PREPARATION:
Make at least twenty photocopies of the "Sheep" pattern (p. 23). (If you prefer, trace the "Sheep" pattern.) Cut out the sheep. Decide where to have your sheep safari—perhaps a park, woodsy area, or your backyard.

Family members will have a great time as they play "hide and go sheep" together.

Just prior to your activity, tape the photocopies of the sheep around the area you've chosen for your safari. Be sure to tape some of the sheep low on bushes or rocks and others higher up on tree trunks or fences. Keep track of how many sheep you "hide."

Gather the family and say: **Oh my! It seems some little sheep have wandered away from their flock. Let's go on a sheep safari and see if we can find every lost sheep in the flock. Look carefully—they could be anywhere!**

Go on a sheep hunt, having family members collect the sheep they find. When all the lost sheep have been found, read Luke 15:4-7. Then ask family members the following questions:

● **How does a good shepherd feel if even one sheep is lost?**
● **Is every lamb important to the flock? Explain.**
● **What does it feel like to be lost? to be found?**

Say: **The Bible tells us that when we wander from God, we** become like lost sheep. But God never wants us to be lost from his flock. If we become lost from God, he searches until he finds us. The Bible also tells us that there is great happiness in heaven when someone is found. So let's share some family happiness with these yummy marshmallow "sheep."

As everyone enjoys a sweet treat of marshmallows, encourage each family member to tell about a time he or she was lost and how it felt to be found. Point out that each of us is important to God and that God is sad if we become lost. Explain that God sends people to help lead us back to him when we become lost.

Encourage family members to use their paper sheep as Bible bookmarks to remind them that God searches for us when we're lost.

terrific tip
If all your children are older, you may want to put a three-minute time limit on searching for the lost sheep. This will add a sense of excitement and challenge to the game.

SHEEP

Instant Picnic

Families will realize that together-times don't need lots of planning—just lots of love.

BIBLE CONCEPT:
We can spend time with God any time, any place.

SCRIPTURE BASIS:
Psalm 121:5-8; 1 Thessalonians 5:17

SUPPLIES:
You'll need a Bible. You'll also need to make a quick family trip to the grocery store for "instant" picnic treats such as crackers, cheese, and fruit; or bread and simple sandwich fixin's.

PREPARATION:
None required.

Spring this together-time on your crew at a moment's notice or any time you're hungry for a light snack or meal.

Pile your family in the car and mysteriously tell them you're going on an adventure, but don't let on where or why you're going. As you drive to the grocery store, ask:

● **What are some things we plan to do every day?**

● **What are some things we do at a moment's notice?**

● **Which is more fun: something that's planned or something we do on a moment's notice? Why?**

At the grocery store, explain that you're going on a special picnic and that everyone is to choose one item he or she would like to take along to share. Suggest that family members choose picnic items such as crackers, fruit, juice, or cheese. Purchase paper towels and cups. When your goodies are gathered, drive to a favorite picnic spot or quiet rest area.

Get your family involved in several simple games such as Freeze Tag, Red Rover, or the age-old classic—Mother, May I? When everyone needs a breather, find a cool spot to sit and to prepare your picnic. Before eating, offer a prayer of thanksgiving for your family and the love and fun you share. As you enjoy your picnic, share memories of fun times you've spent together that weren't planned. Then ask:

- **Why do we need planned together-times? unplanned together-times?**
- **How does sharing fun times express our family's love for each other?**
- **Do we need a planned time to express our love to God? Why or why not?**

Read aloud Psalm 121:5-8 and 1 Thessalonians 5:17. Then ask:

- **What do these verses say about when we can pray to God? why we can pray at any time?**
- **Why do you think God wants us to approach him at any time, planned or unplanned?**

Say: **Sometimes it's fun to share good times and love on the spur of the moment. Because when we love one another, any time is a perfect time to spend together. It's the same way with the time we spend with God. Sometimes we plan time with God, such as when we go to church or when we pray at bedtime. But we can also tell God we love him on the spur of the moment. Because we love God, any time we spend with him is perfect— planned or unplanned!**

Be sure to clean up your picnic area. Then encourage your family to sing a selection of "unplanned" songs to liven up the trip home.

There are few things kids and adults love more than the delight of spontaneity. Look for times to spring spur of the moment activities such as trips to a quick shop, family prayers, fun games, and simple "I love you's" on your family.

The Family Thingamajig

family ♥ goal

Families will discover that communication helps build family understanding.

BIBLE CONCEPT:
God gives us directions that draw us nearer to him.

SCRIPTURE BASIS:
Proverbs 16:9

SUPPLIES:
You'll need a Bible, paper, markers, drinking straws, duct tape, and a variety of building scraps such as wood, plastic pipe, foam, and wire. Check out building sites for colorful (and free!) building "treasures."

PREPARATION:
None required.

Create a bit of cooperative fun as you build solid communication skills between family members.

Place the building scraps, drinking straws, and duct tape in a pile. Then ask family members the following questions:

● **What must someone do to build a building?**

● **What are the most important parts of building something?**

Say: **When something is being built, it's important to have good directions and clear communication. To learn more about**

26

this, let's have some fun building a family "thingamajig"!

Use paper and markers to design a "building plan" for the thingamajig. Then form two groups within your family: the Constructors and the Directors. (It's OK if each "group" has only one member.) Explain that the Directors will give building directions to the Constructors, who will assemble the pieces of your family thingamajig. About halfway through the building process, have groups switch roles. When your thingamajig is complete, discuss the following questions:

● **How did good directions and communication help us build the thingamajig?**

● **What might have happened if we hadn't spoken to one another during the project?**

● **How can talking with family members help build love? trust? our relationship with God?**

Gather around the thingamajig and read aloud Proverbs 16:9. Say: **When we have good communication with God, it helps us hear his directions for our lives. And just as communication with God helps direct his will, communicating with family members helps us know what direction our family is taking. That way we're all on the same track and moving in the right direction.**

End your together-time with a prayer. Join hands around the thingamajig, and offer a prayer thanking God for the gift of talking with our families and with him. Ask God to help your family look for ways to build honest communication. Then end with a corporate "amen."

terrific tip

This activity is especially fun if you have the opportunity to visit a building site (such as a house) and use scrap material found discarded on the ground around the building. Saturday mornings are good times to plan a building excursion, but it's important to get permission from the builder before your special day!

Animal Antics

family ♥ goal:

Family members will learn that all families have the same basic needs, including love and acceptance.

BIBLE CONCEPT:
God provides for everyone, including families.

SCRIPTURE BASIS:
Matthew 6:25-32

SUPPLIES:
You'll need markers, tape, yarn, and one photocopy of the "Family Needs" game sheet (p. 30) for each family member.

PREPARATION:
Tape a twenty-four-inch loop of yarn to a marker. Prepare one "marker necklace" for each family member. For younger children, you may wish to punch holes in the "Family Needs" game sheets and thread them onto the necklaces with the markers.

T his funtabulous activity combines the search-and-find fun of a scavenger hunt with the excitement of a trip to a farm or animal park.

Before your together-time, choose a location that has animals to observe. Petting zoos, farms, regular zoos, animal shelters, or local game preserves all work equally well.

On the way to your destination, get family members excited about your trip and thinking about various needs by playing the game I'm Going to the Zoo. Have one person begin the game by saying, "I'm going to the zoo, and I need to take a...(fill in a need)." Then have the next person repeat the sentence and add his or her own need. Continue until each person has added several needs.

When you arrive at your destination, hand everyone a copy of the "Family Needs" game sheet and a marker necklace to wear around his or her neck. Explain that this game is all about finding out what animal families and human families need. Tell your family that when one of them observes an animal need pictured on the game

28

sheet, he or she can write an X on that need and on the corresponding need for humans. When someone makes a tic-tac-toe, that
person can give another family member a high five.

As you explore the different animals and animal families, which
may also include birds and fish, make comments such as "Animal
families have many needs just as human families do" and "God provides for animals just as he provides for people."

When your animal adventure is over and you're on the return
trip, compare your "Family Needs" game sheets to see if everyone
found which needs animal families and human families have in com-
mon. Then ask:

● **How are the needs of animal families and human families
alike? different?**

● **In what ways does God meet the needs of animal families?
human families?**

● **How can we help meet our own family needs for food?
shelter? love? acceptance?**

Say: **Both humans and animals need food, shelter, and protection. But human families need an extra helping of love and
acceptance, too. Isn't it great that God loves us enough to provide for all our needs?**

Wrap up your trip by inviting each family member to complete
the following sentence: "I'm going home with my family, and I need to
take…" End the sentence with phrases such as "lots of hugs," "love and
acceptance," or "thank you's to God for my family."

terrific tip
Make a family needs display by inviting family members
to draw either a picture of one need they observed at
the zoo or one need in your family. Tape the pictures to a
sheet of poster board and label it "God provides for our needs." Hang
the poster in a place where it will remind everyone to thank God for
his special "family provisions."

29

Family Needs

When you observe one of the animal family needs depicted in the top tic-tac-toe grid, write an X on that picture and a second X on the corresponding human family need in the lower tic-tac-toe grid.

Book Party Pizazz!

Families will find out that each family member is a unique individual.

BIBLE CONCEPT:
God created each one of us special.

SCRIPTURE BASIS:
Psalm 139:14

SUPPLIES:
You'll need a Bible, markers, uninflated balloons, graham crackers, colorful sprinkles, canned icing, plastic knives, and plates. You'll also need photocopies of the "Book Party Pizazz" invitation on page 33.

PREPARATION:
Copy the "Book Party Pizazz" invitation on brightly colored paper, one invitation for each family member. Tape an uninflated balloon to each invitation. (Use a different color balloon for each family member, if possible.) To add an extra festive touch, provide colorful paper plates for the party snacks.

This simple—and simply sensational—party idea takes family members on an imaginary adventure—all through the wonder of books.

Before party time, hand each family member a party invitation. Help younger children read the invitations and explain that they're to choose a favorite storybook to share with everyone in the family. Expect squeals of delight and a difficult time choosing just one book to share. If your family is very small, let children choose two reading treasures to share. Parents may want to bring along their favorite book to tell about, but they should also choose the child's book they most enjoy reading aloud at bedtime.

When party time arrives, place the party treats on a low table near your reading area. Then gather everyone, and invite them to display their books on the floor by the table. When everyone is comfy-cozy on their "reading" pillows, invite family members to tell a bit about the books they brought. Encourage children to tell the title of the book and why they enjoy it so much.

To decide whose book will be read first, have everyone blow up his or her balloon and pinch it shut. When you give the signal, family members are to let their balloons sail across the room. The person whose balloon travels farthest shares his or her book first. If that person is too young to read, let him or her choose a family member to read aloud the book.

After several books have been read, ask the following questions:
- **Why do you think we all like different books? different colors? different foods?**
- **Who do you think created us to be so unique and special?**

Hold up the Bible and say: **The Bible is a special book that God wants us to read every day and to share with others—just as we've shared our favorite books. The Bible tells us that God created each of us special. That's why we have different likes and dislikes.** Read aloud Psalm 139:14. Then ask:
- **What would it be like if we all liked the same things?**
- **How can we tell God we're glad that each of us is special?**

Finish sharing the books everyone brought along. Then invite family members to decorate graham cracker "books" to nibble and enjoy. As you decorate the crackers, point out how everyone adds different ingredients to his or her treat and how everyone's edible book looks different. Remind family members that it's fun to share different likes and dislikes and that everyone is special because of them.

End your party by blowing up and tying off the balloons. Then draw smiles on each other's balloons to show how happy you are that each family member is a special individual.

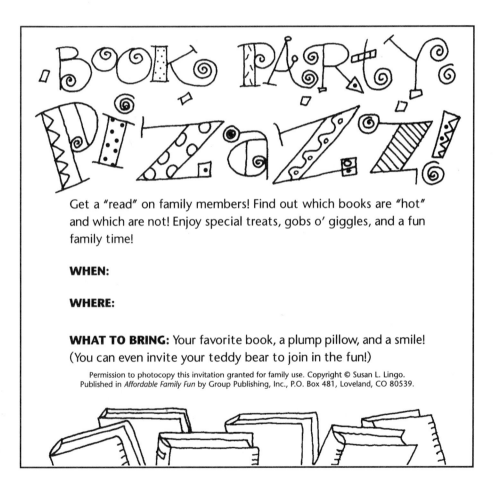

terrific tip

Kids love receiving mail addressed to them! Consider mailing each child's party invitation several days prior to the big event. Then sit back and smile as children excitedly await your special family party.

BOOK PARTY PIZAZZ!

Get a "read" on family members! Find out which books are "hot" and which are not! Enjoy special treats, gobs o' giggles, and a fun family time!

WHEN:

WHERE:

WHAT TO BRING: Your favorite book, a plump pillow, and a smile! (You can even invite your teddy bear to join in the fun!)

Bubblin' With Love

Families will learn that following God keeps them close and headed in the same direction.

BIBLE CONCEPT:
God wants us to follow him together.

SCRIPTURE BASIS:
Philippians 2:1-2

SUPPLIES:
You'll need a container of soap bubbles and a blowing wand for each family member.

PREPARATION:
Purchase plastic jars of ready-made soap bubbles or prepare the recipe below to make homemade bubbles. For a fun selection of bubble wands, use squares of mesh screen, bend twist-tie wires or chenille wires into different shapes, or use pop-can rings for older kids.

Sudsy Soap Bubbles

Mix 1 teaspoon white corn syrup, 1/3 cup dish-washing liquid (Joy or Dawn works best), 1 cup water, and 1 teaspoon sugar. Stir mixture until the sugar dissolves. Then pour into individual cups to use as bubble-blowing solution.

A breezy, sunny day and shimmery soap bubbles make this delightful devotion a real winner for even the tiniest tots—while teaching the entire family about following God.

Hand each family member a container of soap bubbles and a bubble-blowing wand. Go outside and invite the bubbles and your family's imaginations to fly free and high as you experiment with bubble blowing. Challenge your family to blow huge bubbles, tiny bubbles, bubble-bunches, and more. After several minutes, say: **Let's try something different! When I count to three, everyone blow one bubble, and let's watch to see where the bubbles go.** Count to three and watch the bubbles sail away together in the breeze. Then ask:

- **Where did our bubbles go?**
- **Why did they float away in the same direction?**
- **What do you think would happen if we blew bubbles in different directions?**

Try blowing bubbles as you stand with your backs together. Watch where the bubbles fly, then ask:

- **What happened to our bubbles?**
- **Why did the bubbles stay together even when we blew them in different directions?**

Say: **Our bubbles traveled in the same direction and stayed together because they were following the breeze. Did you know that's a lot like following God? When our family follows God, we stay together and travel in the same direction. That means our family works together, helps one another, loves each other, prays together, and even has fun together—just like now! When we love and follow God, we stay together and go in the same direction.**

Continue your bubble blowing escapades and try some of the following ideas for even more family fun.

- Play Bubble Addition with partners. Try to get one bubble to join with another to make a double-bubble. Then blow a third bubble to join the other two and so on.
- Blow bubbles in different directions such as upside down, under

your elbows, lying on the ground, and as you twirl around.

● Play a zany game of Bubble Bash by having one person blow bubbles and call out a way to pop them, such as "with your thumbs" or "with your ears." Family members then run to pop bubbles in the chosen way.

terrific tip

Turn this fun family devotion into a creative family craft. Simply add a bit of food coloring to the soap, and blow bubbles onto white paper. When the bubbles pop, they'll leave a beautiful splotch of shimmery color to remind you of your great together-time.

Deck the Yard

Families will discover that serving others is serving God.

BIBLE CONCEPT:
God wants us to be cheerful servants.

SCRIPTURE BASIS:
Psalm 100:2; 2 Corinthians 9:7-9

SUPPLIES:
You'll need a Bible, plastic lawn bags; flower seeds or bedding plants; colorful silk, plastic, or paper flowers; and yard tools such as rakes and trowels.

PREPARATION:
Choose an elderly or disabled neighbor's yard as your project site. Be sure to ask this person's permission for your family to do some spring-time raking and planting. If you're planning to use paper flowers, let your family go wild by creating colorful blossoms from neon poster board, then securely taping the flowers to plastic drinking straws.

Watch smiles blossom with flowers in this springtime family service project.

Gather for a family meeting and ask the following questions:

- **How does it feel to do something nice for someone?**
- **What are some different ways we can serve others?**
- **How does serving others show them our love? show God our love?**

Read aloud 2 Corinthians 9:7-9 and Psalm 100:2. Then say: **There are lots of ways to serve others and show them that we care. We can serve through our prayers or donations of money—even through giving our time and talents. God likes it when we serve others and do nice things for them, so let's do something fun on this springtime day. We can serve one of our neighbors by making his or her yard especially pretty for springtime!**

Explain that family members can rake grass and leaves and plant pretty flowers around the yard—while serving your neighbor and God at the same time.

When you arrive at your neighbor's yard, take turns raking, bagging, and planting. Plant real flowers or flower seeds in pretty locations, or stick paper flowers in the ground around the front yard to make it springtime festive. As you work, remind your family that God is smiling at their handiwork and love. Point out that serving others also means you're serving God and that God will enjoy the bright flowers and clean yard as much as your neighbor!

When you're through "decking the yard," be sure to dispose of any lawn bags.

terrific tip
If your family wants to take this springtime service project one step further, let them decorate ready-made cookies with canned icing and gumdrop flowers. Then wrap the colorful goodies in plastic wrap and add a bow and a slip of paper with 2 Corinthians 9:8 written on it. Present this special treat to your neighbor when you've finished decking the yard with love!

Bus Boarding

Families will find out that the straightest path
to God is through Jesus.

BIBLE CONCEPT:
Jesus is the straight path to God.

SCRIPTURE BASIS:
John 14:6

SUPPLIES:
You'll need a Bible, paper, and crayons.

PREPARATION:
Check local bus schedules to see when and where the nearest bus travels. Make plans to ride the bus on a particular day. If there is no bus in your area, take a drive in the family car and pretend that you're taking the bus on a special trip!

Young children who have never experienced a bus ride will adore this unusual family activity—and powerful lesson about Jesus.

Put paper, crayons, and the Bible in a tote bag or sack. Take your family to the bus stop or gather in the family car. Explain that this adventure is all about paths and roads and twists and turns. Hand each person a sheet of paper and a crayon or marker.

Tell family members that, as they ride the bus, they're to "draw" their paths. Starting with their crayons in the center of the paper, they are to make a curved line each time the bus turns a corner. When the round trip is complete, papers should be covered with one long squiggly design! During the trip, family members can exchange colors, but they must begin to draw at the place they left off with the last color.

As you ride, make comments such as "My, this bus is making a lot of turns and twists" and "What if we went in a straight line instead of making so many turns?" Encourage everyone to keep drawing "turns" on the paper each time the bus rounds a corner. Have older children who know their left and right directions actually draw lines to the left

38

or right to match the bus driver's turning directions.

At the end of your trip, disembark and find a place to relax for a few moments. Compare your designs and ask:

● **With so many turns to remember, what might happen if a bus driver takes the wrong turn?**

● **Which do you think is shorter and easier: to make many turns or to travel in a straight line? Explain.**

Say: **The Bible tells us that traveling in a straight path is the best way to heaven. When we go in the straight direction that God sets out, we avoid dangers and becoming lost. Let's read what else the Bible says about the best pathway to God. When you hear what that way is, put your hand on your heart.**

Read aloud John 14:6. Then ask:

● **Who is the straight path to God?**

● **How can following the straight path with Jesus keep us from making wrong turns and getting lost?**

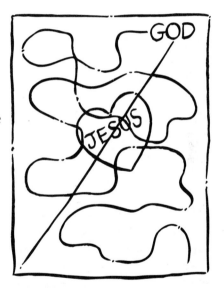

Have each family member draw a large heart shape in the center of the paper and write the word "Jesus" in the heart. Then ask each one to draw a straight diagonal line across the paper and write "GOD" in a corner where the line ends. Invite family members to display their pathway designs on a wall to remind them that the only straight path to God is through Jesus.

terrific tip

For an even more colorful touch, let children paint over their crayon designs with watercolor paints. The crayon wax will resist the paint and make the pictures even more beautiful for displaying in your "family art gallery!"

Bird Walk, Family Talk

family ♥ *goal:*

Families will learn the importance of staying
on the right path to God.

BIBLE CONCEPT:
It's important to follow God.

SCRIPTURE BASIS:
John 15:10

SUPPLIES:
You'll need a Bible, paper lunch sacks, markers, and crayons. Also gather up some "bird goodies" such as stale crackers, cereal, bread, or croutons.

PREPARATION:
None required.

Kids will love following the unusual path in this outside together-time—and offering birds a tasty banquet!

Set out markers and crayons. Give each family member a paper lunch sack. Say: **Let's play a game of Follow the Leader. I'll draw a simple design on my sack, and you follow by drawing the same design on yours. Then someone else can draw a design for the rest of us to follow.** Continue drawing and following designs until everyone has had a chance to lead. Then ask:

• **Why is it important to be a good follower?**
• **Who are some people we want to follow?**

Say: **Let's see if we can be good followers on a very unusual path.** Set out the selection of stale crackers, cereal, and bread and let each family member fill his or her sack half full. Then lead your family outside or go to a nearby park. Explain that everyone can drop crumbs on the ground to make a path to a designated landmark, such as a particular bush, tree, or playground apparatus. When all the goodies are deposited, have family members try to follow the

40

paths that others made. Then gather everyone in a group. Ask:

- **How can paths help us get where we want to go?**
- **What might happen if we wandered off the path?**
- **Why is it important to follow God and the paths he lays out for us?**

Say: **God wants us to be his good followers because God knows that when we stay on the path that leads to him, our family won't get lost. How can we stay on the right path and follow God?** Let family members tell their ideas, which might include reading the Bible, praying, helping each other, and showing love to one another.

Then say: **You know, the paths we made will make a lot of hungry birds happy. And just as our path will feed the birds, God feeds us when we're on the path to him. God feeds us with his love, care, and protection—and that makes us happy! Let's follow our paths once more to remind us that we always want to follow God.**

On the trip home, lead your family in singing "I Have Decided to Follow Jesus." If you're walking on your trip, let each family member have a turn leading the others in skipping, walking on tiptoes, walking backward, or jogging. When you return home, read aloud John 15:10 and talk together about the importance of following God and obeying him.

terrific tip

Keep the decorated paper sacks, and encourage your family to write or draw pictures of ways they can follow God during the upcoming week. Place the pictures in the sacks, then share which ways you followed God at the end of the week.

Home-Spun Fun

Things to Do & Make at Home

You're GREAT!

It "Ads" Up!

family ♥ goal:

*Families will learn that it's important to recognize
each family member with genuine love.*

BIBLE CONCEPT:
We're all important to God.

SCRIPTURE BASIS:
Titus 3:4-7

SUPPLIES:
You'll need a Bible, newspaper, sheets of poster board, construction
paper, glue sticks, and slips of paper. You'll also need a variety of decorating supplies such as markers, crayons, glitter glue, stickers,
bingo daubers, and ribbon.

PREPARATION:
Write each family member's name on a separate slip of
paper, then fold the papers in half.

This affirming art project gives warm fuzzies—and worthwhile
credit—to each family member.

Cover a hard floor with newspapers, then set out the poster
board and craft supplies. Place the slips of paper beside you. Call
family members, clapping as each person gathers around the craft
items. Encourage everyone to join in the clapping as each person
arrives. When everyone is present, ask:

● **Why do people clap for each other?**

● **How do you feel when someone recognizes you're special?**

Say: **Sometimes we forget how truly special each person in
our family is. We forget to tell or show them how much they
mean to us. So let's take some time to express our love and
appreciation for our family. Choose a slip of paper with someone's name on it. If you draw your own name, hand it to me and
I'll mix it back in with the other names. Otherwise, keep that
name a secret! Then decorate a special poster or advertisement
telling everyone how great that person is!**

44

Let everyone choose a name slip. Read and whisper the names for very young children. If you have older children, talk about things that are included in product advertisements, such as how great a product is, what it does, and how it makes people's lives really wonderful. Then encourage family members to create colorful ads for the people whose names they drew. Young children will especially enjoy making colorful "You're Great!" posters.

As your family works on their secret projects, make comments such as "Our family has so much fun together! That's because each one of us is so special" and "God loves every person in our family so much!"

When the projects are complete, turn them over to keep them secret. Then ask a family member to read aloud Titus 3:4-7. Ask:

- **According to these verses, who does God love, care for, and appreciate?**

- **How does it feel to know God treasures everyone—even when we don't deserve it?**

- **Why is it important to let family members know how great we think they are?**

Invite each person to present his or her poster or advertisement to the family member for whom it was created. Have the artist tell the "honoree" how much he or she is loved and appreciated, then give that person a warm hug. Encourage everyone to clap and cheer. Continue until all the advertisements and posters have been warmly presented. Then hang the colorful affirmations in places where they'll be noticed—and the people appreciated—often.

Family Box Bowling

family ♥ goal:

Families will discover that loving each other is full of fun.

BIBLE CONCEPT:
Loving one another makes us feel happy.

SCRIPTURE BASIS:
John 15:17

SUPPLIES:
You'll need a Bible, various medium-sized boxes, six paper cups, markers, and soft "bowling" balls made from pairs of rolled socks. You'll need one bowling ball for each family member. Be sure the bowling balls will roll through the boxes easily.

PREPARATION:
None required.

H ave a family blast on a rainy day—or any day—with this "get-the-fun-rolling" game.

Set out the paper cups, boxes, and markers. Invite family members to color three paper cups red and three blue. Number the paper cup bowling "pins" in each set one, two, and three. Then cut or tear the ends off the boxes to make "tunnels." Use the boxes, cups, and sock balls to play a variety of unique bowling games from the selections below.

TUNNEL BOWLING—Line up both sets of paper cup bowling pins at one end of the room, alternating colors. Have family members stand at the opposite end of the room. Place the box tunnels in the center of the room with openings facing the bowling pins and players. Explain that family members are to roll their sock balls through the tunnels to bowl over the pins. When a bowling pin is downed, the Roller gives another family member a high five. Continue until all the pins are bowled over. Older kids may enjoy an extra challenge of trying to knock over only red or only blue pins, or you may form family teams and assign each team a color to bowl over. If an opponent's color is toppled, a pin from the roller's team must be set up as a "penalty play."

BOWL ME OVER—Hand each family member a bowling pin and a sock ball. Have players spread out within the room and stand beside their pins to guard them from being bowled over by an opponent. Players are to roll their sock balls and try to knock over someone else's pin. If someone's pin is toppled, he or she shouts, "Bull's-eye!" Any player with a toppled pin can continue trying to roll over other bowling pins. Continue until only one pin remains standing.

COUNT-TO-TEN BOWLING—Form pairs and hand each pair one bowling pin and one sock ball. Have partners stand facing each other about fifteen feet apart with their bowling pin between them. On "Go," have partners roll the sock balls back and forth trying to topple their own pins. Each time a pin is toppled, count one point and run to reset the pin. Continue until each pair reaches ten points. If younger children are playing, you may wish to count to five instead. Older kids might enjoy "counting" their way though the alphabet or books of the Bible.

When you're ready for a bowling break, gather the family and read aloud John 15:17. Then ask:

- What's the best part about having fun as a family?
- How do you feel when our family is having a good time?
- How do you think God feels when our family has fun?
- How does spending fun together-times help family love grow?

Say: **When a family loves each other, they naturally want to spend time together. And playing games is a great way to show how much fun loving each other can be. That's a lot like loving God. It's fun to love God because he teaches us and keeps us safe—and loves us back sooo much! Fun and love go together just as families and fun go together. So let's have more family fun by bowling another game.**

terrific tip

If your children are young and lack the motor skills to accurately roll the sock balls, turn the boxes on their sides so the openings face upward. Then let children toss the sock balls into the boxes like beanbags.

Pillow Talk

family ♥ goal:

Families will recognize the importance of family prayer.

BIBLE CONCEPT:
God wants us to pray for our families.

SCRIPTURE BASIS:
Philippians 4:6; 1 Thessalonians 5:16-18; James 5:16

SUPPLIES:
You'll need a Bible, a bag of polyester fiberfill, permanent markers, and two eight-inch squares of craft felt for each family member. You'll also need needles, thread, and scissors. If your children are a bit older, add scraps of colorful fabric and tacky craft glue to your supplies.

PREPARATION:
None required.

This creative family project is as inspiring as it is "crafty"—and perfect for a Saturday evening together.

Set out the craft supplies, and gather the family. Then have family members discuss the following questions:

- **What is prayer?**
- **Why is it important to pray?**
- **Who are we to pray for? Why?**

Say: **Let's see what the Bible says about prayer.** Ask for several volunteers to read aloud these Scriptures: James 5:16; 1 Thessalonians 5:16-18; and Philippians 4:6. Then ask:

- **What kinds of things are we to pray for?**
- **What happens when we pray for others? for our family?**
- **Why is it important to pray for our family?**

Say: **God wants us to talk to him, and that's just what we do when we pray. We talk to God and tell him what makes us happy and sad, and what things we need and want for ourselves and others. It's very important to pray for our family needs, too. When we pray for our family and the people in our family, it shows God how much we love our family. It's also a good way to thank God for each person in our family. So let's make special Prayer Pillows to remind us to pray for our family.**

Let each person choose two felt squares and decorate one square with markers and colorful felt shapes. Then have each family member sign his or her name on all the undecorated felt squares. When everyone has signed each other's plain felt square, help each other hold the two squares together and stitch around the sides of the squares, leaving several inches in which to stuff fiberfill. (You can also use tacky craft glue or staples to attach the sides of the felt squares. If you use staples, be sure to cover them with colorful vinyl tape.) After stuffing the "pillow" with fiberfill, finish by stitching the opening. Encourage family members to display their Prayer Pillows.

Gather family members in a circle. Hold up a Prayer Pillow, and explain that you'll toss the Prayer Pillow to someone across the circle and say, "I'll pray for (person's name)." Then that person can toss the Prayer Pillow to someone and repeat the sentence. Continue until everyone in the family has been named. Then end with a family prayer thanking God for your family and asking God to help everyone remember to pray for the family each day. Have family members place their Prayer Pillows on their beds to remind them to include the family in their nighttime prayers.

terrific tip

If you have very young children, let your child "sleep" on his or her prayers. Remind your child that God never sleeps because he is busy loving and protecting his people—and answering their prayers.

The Fabulous Family Diner

family ♥ goal:

Families will discover that it's important to serve each other.

BIBLE CONCEPT:
When we serve others, we're serving God.

SCRIPTURE BASIS:
Matthew 25:40

SUPPLIES:

You'll need cubed fresh fruits, cleaned raw vegetables, a prepared pizza crust, pretzel sticks, toothpicks, and pizza toppings such as sauce, cheese, mushrooms, pepperoni, olives, and green peppers. You'll also need plates, napkins, and chilled beverages.

PREPARATION:

This dinnertime devotion involves food preparation as part of the activity, but you'll need to cube the fruits and clean the vegetables as described above.

This funky "diner" will keep family members coming back for seconds—and serving one another with smiles and grrreat service!

Gather family members and say: **Tonight we'll have some fun with the grand opening of our Fabulous Family Diner. This cool diner specializes in funky food, super service, and miles of smiles! You're invited to serve one another by making and enjoying some great food and fun!**

Have family members choose which part of the menu they'd like to prepare: Funky-Fruit Kabobs, the Monster Veggie Sculpture, or the Perfect Pizza. Make the Funky-Fruit Kabobs by sliding chunks of fruit on pretzel sticks. Prepare the Monster Veggie Sculpture by attaching raw vegetables together with toothpicks. And make the Perfect Pizza by spreading pizza sauce on prepared pizza crust and adding any variety of toppings in an interesting design. Bake the pizza under adult supervision until done.

As dinner is cooking, read aloud Matthew 25:40. Then ask:

● **Why is it important to help and to serve each other?**

● **What does it mean that when we serve others, we're serving God?**

● **Why do you think God wants us to serve the people in our own family?**

● **How can serving one another bring us closer to God? to each other?**

Say: **We know that it's important to help others, but sometimes we forget to help and serve the people in our own family.
Did you know that when you serve the people in our family
you're also serving God? That's right! The Bible tells us that
serving others is a way of serving God, too. Now let's serve each
other a delicious meal at our Fabulous Family Diner!**

Get into pairs or trios and serve each other by carrying plates to
the table. Then offer a family prayer thanking God for the good food,
your family, and the chance to serve each other and God.

terrific tip Adding several "cool" touches such as a red-checked
tablecloth, a menu board, Coca-Cola glasses, and '50s
music will make your family diner the "place to eat for a
memorable treat!"

House of Love

family ♥ goal:

*Families will learn that a house is a home
only when love lives inside.*

BIBLE CONCEPT:
God's homes are filled with love.

SCRIPTURE BASIS:
John 14:1-4

SUPPLIES:
You'll need a Bible, a roll of white shelf paper, pencils with erasers,
and blue felt-tip pens.

PREPARATION:
Cut a two-foot length of shelf paper for each family member.

This creative family activity centers around building plans for "dream" houses—and for loving homes.

Set out the pencils and pens, then hand each person a sheet of white shelf paper. Ask:

- **If you could build your "dream" house, what would it be like?**
- **How would your dream house be different from any other house? How would it be similar?**

Challenge family members to use their imaginations to create blueprints for their dream houses. Have family members design and draw their plans on paper in pencil and then trace the final design in blue pen. As your family works and plans, talk about the features that might make for great houses, such as cozy fireplaces, family rooms, and roomy kitchens where everyone shares delicious dinners. Ask questions such as "What makes a house more than just a building to live in?" and "In addition to room design, what other things are important to homes?"

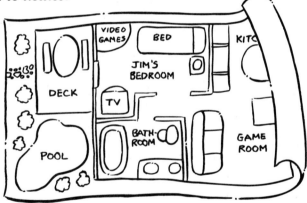

When the building plans are complete, invite each "architect" to give the family a "tour" of his or her design. Compare and contrast how the houses are similar and different. Then say: **These building plans for houses are wonderful, but I have an important question for all you architects: What makes a house a "home"?** Encourage family members to discuss what makes a building into a real home. Answers might include caring people, warmth, acceptance, and love. Then say: **There is a big difference between just staying in a building and living in a loving home. Let's see what the Bible says about homes.** Invite family members to take turns reading aloud John 14:1-4. Then ask:

- What do you think will make our home in heaven so special?
- How can love make the house we live in a special home?
- In what ways are loving homes similar to what our home in heaven will be like?
- How does a loving home bring us closer to God? to each other? to others?

Have everyone write on his or her building plan one thing that makes a house a home, such as love, caring, acceptance, or loving God. Then hang the building plans throughout your own loving home to remind everyone that "bricks build a house—but *love* builds a home!"

terrific tip Families with young children will enjoy using building blocks instead of paper to design their dream houses. Use a variety of building blocks and other materials such as boxes, paper cups, and empty soda pop cans to create happening houses and fun "family frame-ups"!

Honor Your Family!

family goal:

Families will realize that each family member deserves recognition.

BIBLE CONCEPT:
God recognizes each of us because we're special in his eyes.

SCRIPTURE BASIS:
Deuteronomy 7:6

SUPPLIES:
You'll need a Bible, poster board, tape, balloons, markers, slips of paper, pencils, drinking straws, curly ribbons, and a box of colorful note cards with envelopes.

PREPARATION:
None required until the day you've chosen as each person's "Recognition Night."

This special family activity turns cool evenings into warm nights of recognition—and family members into real "stars"!

Choose one night a week as Family Recognition Night, then devote one evening to each family member. This requires a bit of planning and may spread out over a month or more to allow each person his or her own special night—but the extra effort is well worth it!

For each family member's Recognition Night, have everyone else help prepare the following items.

PERSONAL POSTER—Have family members secretly prepare a poster or hanging mobile featuring the family member who is to be recognized. Use magazines to cut out his or her favorite foods, fashions, or cars. Glue photographs of the honoree to the poster. You might even attach several coupons to the poster for special treats such as doughnuts, a carwash, or a free movie rental. Make each poster as personalized as possible!

NIFTY NOTES—Supply each family member not being honored with a note card on which to draw pictures or write personal notes to the honoree. Slip the Nifty Notes into decorated envelopes, and then hide the envelopes around the room on the honoree's special night.

MESSAGE BALLOONS—Have each family member prepare an "I love you, and you're special because..." message. Write the simple messages on narrow slips of paper that can be inserted into uninflated balloons. Then blow up and tie off the balloons. Tape the balloons to drinking straws or pencils to create a unique "balloon bouquet." Add curly ribbon for an extra-special touch.

When the time arrives to recognize the honoree, escort him or her to a distinguished place, such as a favorite chair, and present him or her with the Personal Poster and bouquet of Message Balloons. Then invite the honoree to search for the collection of Nifty Notes. You may wish to serve the honoree's favorite dessert, then gather as the family relates humorous, loving, or otherwise special memories of this honored family member. End by reading aloud Deuteronomy 7:6 and saying a prayer for the honoree, thanking God for his or her place in your family and in God's family.

terrific tip Don't overlook grandparents in this great devotional idea! You may need to wait until Grandma and Grandpa come for a visit, but kids will treasure the chance to express their love and respect for these members of your family.

No-Scowl Towels

family ♥ goal:

Families will discover that happiness is a choice.

BIBLE CONCEPT:
God wants us to be joyful.

SUPPLIES:
You'll need a Bible, newspaper, paint pens or squirt bottles of fabric paint, and a package of inexpensive terry cloth washcloths. You'll need one washcloth for each family member.
PREPARATION:
None required.

F amily members will enjoy using these cheery "towels" to wash their faces—and put smiles in their hearts.

Cover a table with newspapers and set out the paints and terry washcloths. Ask:

● **When was a time you felt like a cranky grump-monster for no reason?**

● **How does being cranky affect our family? How does being cheerful affect us?**

Say: **There are times when we're unhappy or grumpy and take out those cranky feelings on family members. Without meaning to, we may hurt someone's feelings or make that person feel sad. It's not possible to be happy all the time, but we can choose how we let our feelings affect others. Happiness and treating others with joyful kindness is a choice we make. And when we love God, that choice is much easier! Let's see what the Bible says about happiness.** Invite someone to read aloud Philippians 4:4. Then have family members discuss the following questions:

- **What happens when you're around someone who's happy?**
- **Why do you think that happiness is "catching"?**
- **How does choosing to love God help us choose to be happy?**

Say: **Every day, we can choose whether to be cranky, sad, or happy. And when we love God, it's much easier to choose happiness. That way, even when things go wrong, we feel the joy of loving God! So let's make some "No-Scowl Towels" to remind us that each morning we can make the right choice to start the day with a smile on our faces—and in our hearts.**

Give each person a terry cloth washcloth and invite him or her to decorate one side using fabric paint. Encourage everyone to make "happy" designs such as smiley faces, hearts, flowers, and playful squiggles. Be sure to have everyone personalize his or her towel by adding a signature or initials. As you work, talk about times when a smile or frown was catching and which was nicer to be around.

When you finish, gather around your No-Scowl Towels and thank God for the gift of his love and joy. Allow the cloths to dry overnight before using them.

terrific tip If you want to avoid the possibility of messy paints with very young children, simply use colorful permanent markers instead of fabric paint. And remember—these cute and colorful towels make great gifts that even the youngest family members can make for Grandma and Grandpa!

Terrific Tents

family ♥ goal:

Families will discover that God provides different places for families to live.

BIBLE CONCEPT:
God takes care of us in different ways.

SUPPLIES:
You'll need a variety of household "building materials" such as pillows, bedsheets, blankets, beach towels, tables, and chairs. You'll also want a large candle and matches.

PREPARATION:
None required.

This fun family activity is most enjoyed by parents and young children.

Set out a supply of large bedsheets, blankets, and beach towels in the family room, living room, or den. Set the candle and matches aside. Invite family members to come for an afternoon or evening of indoor "camping" fun. Have everyone bring his or her favorite pillow, teddy bear, or other stuffed animal.

When everyone has arrived, challenge family members to build their own special tents using pillows, sheets, blankets, towels, tables, and chairs. You may wish to let children use cushions from old chairs or sofas for "giant" building blocks. For a really neat touch, play a bit of lively music or an outdoor sound effects tape during "camp setup."

When everyone's tent is complete, place the unlit candle in the center of the room or in a spot near all the "campers." Invite each family member to take everyone on a "tour" of his or her tent. Then gather everyone around the candle "campfire" and ask:

● **In what ways are our tent-homes alike? different?**
● **Why do you think some families live in tents?**
● **Where are some other places that families live?**
● **Who provides a place for us to live as well as food to eat and fresh water to drink?**

Say: **God is our great provider. He provides places for families to live and materials with which we build our homes. Some families live in tents; others live in houses or apartments or condominiums. In other places, families live in caves or grass huts or even in igloos made of ice! God loves us and wants us to be safe and dry and warm, so he provides materials for family homes. Let's say a prayer around the campfire and thank God for the house we live in and for providing all we need to live.**

Light the candle, and offer a prayer of thanks to God. Encourage each family member to say a word of thanks about the place in which you live. Then have fun "camping" out by reading stories around your makeshift campfire, playing Who's In the Tent? and listening to soft music or jungle sounds. If this is a nighttime activity, invite family members to sleep in their tents.

terrific tip

If you have a family-sized tent and a warm summer night, consider a night of backyard camping under the stars. Use a small grill for a "campfire" and roast marshmallows for a special treat.

Welcome to Our Home

family ♥ goal:

Families will learn that welcoming others into the family home honors God.

BIBLE CONCEPT:
God wants us to welcome others.

SCRIPTURE BASIS:
Joshua 24:15 (New Century Version)

60

SUPPLIES:

You'll need a Bible, wide satin ribbon, different colors of thick yarn or ribbon, scissors, and a large jingle bell for each person. You'll also need one photocopy of the verse box on page 62.

PREPARATION:

Cut nine two-foot lengths of yarn or ribbon for each family member. Keep several feet of yarn or ribbon for later use. Cut an eighteen-inch length of wide satin ribbon. Photocopy the verse box (p. 62) on stiff paper and cut it out.

T his colorful front door chime lets visitors know you welcome them into your home—and God into your lives.

Set out the pieces of yarn or ribbon, the scissors, the jingle bells, and the wide ribbon. Gather family members and ask:

● **When is a time you felt really welcome in someone's home?**

● **How did it feel when you were welcomed in such a nice way?**

● **Why is it important to make guests feel welcome in our home?**

● **How does making someone feel welcome show our love for God?**

Explain that the family will work together to make a beautiful welcome chime for the front door. Have older children and adults each knot nine lengths of yarn or ribbon at the top, divide the "streamers" into groups of three, and braid these groups together down the length of yarn or ribbon. Tie the braids or twists several inches from the bottom and allow the ends to hang like fringe.

Help young children knot nine lengths of yarn or ribbon at the top, twist a few inches of yarn and knot it, then twist and knot down the length of yarn. Or have young children simply layer the colors of yarn or ribbon and tie them into one large loop.

When the braids, twists, or loops are done, they should be thick and colorful. Help each family member cut a six-inch piece of yarn or ribbon and tie his or her jingle bell somewhere onto the braid, twist, or loop. Then shake the bells and listen to the joyous music your family makes together!

Read aloud Joshua 24:15 from the Bible or the verse box. Then ask the following questions and encourage family members to shake their jingle bells when they'd like a turn to talk.

● **Who should our family always want to serve?**
● **How is welcoming others into our home a good way to serve God?**

Join the braids, twists, and loops at the top by tying them together in a bow with the wide satin ribbon. Tie or tape the verse box to the bow. Now hang your family door chime on the front door to cheerfully welcome guests and herald to all whom your family serves.

terrific tip Let children make additional braids or twists to hang on bedroom doors to welcome their own special friends or to give door chimes to favorite relatives as a unique gifts.

"As for me and my family, we will serve the Lord."

JOSHUA 24:15c

Top-Secret Sweets

family ♥ goal:

Families will discover that together they can make a difference.

BIBLE CONCEPT:
God wants us to be kind to others.

SCRIPTURE BASIS:
Matthew 6:4a; Ephesians 4:32

SUPPLIES:
You'll need a Bible, plastic knives, canned icing, powdered sugar, squeeze icing, plastic bags, paper plates, bows, plastic wrap, and candy decorations such as gumdrops, tiny cinnamon candies, and colorful sprinkles. You'll also need a variety of ready-made cookies such as sugar cookies, sandwich cookies, fig cookies, and graham crackers.

PREPARATION:
None required.

This family service project makes a delightful addition to your Christmas tradition of giving to others.

Set out the ready-made cookies, icing, plastic knives, and candy decorations. Gather the family and ask:

- **When have you secretly done something nice for someone?**
- **How did it make you feel to show kindness in a secret way?**

Read aloud Ephesians 4:32 and Matthew 6:4a, then ask:

- **Why do you think God wants us to show kindness to others?**
- **Why do you think God wants us to do nice things in secret?**
- **Why is it more fun to show kindness to others in secret?**
- **How do you think people who receive "secret kindnesses" feel?**

Say: **We can have some delicious family fun and keep it all top secret! Let's pretend we're cookie-angels in charge of sending love to others through special cookies. We'll decorate lots of delicious delights to secretly share with others. That way we'll spread love**

63

and kindness just the way God wants—without having to receive any rewards except the good feelings we'll enjoy. Use your cookie-angel imaginations to decorate your goodies, then we'll put them on plates with pretty bows to secretly hand out.

Let family members decorate their cookie treats however they wish, or use several of the following suggestions below:

FABULOUS FIGGY DELIGHTS—Sprinkle a bit of powdered sugar on top of each fig cookie or bar, then squirt a bit of icing in the center. Add a small cinnamon candy to the center of the icing. Use green icing for leaves and red candies for holly berries to make lovely holiday treats.

ZEBRAS—Spread thin stripes of white icing across chocolate sandwich cookies. For reverse Zebras, use chocolate icing and vanilla sandwich cookies.

PRETTY PETALS—Use icing to "glue" gumdrop bits to the tops of small sugar cookies to make colorful blossoms. If you have clean craft sticks, sandwich a stick between two small sugar cookies and glue the two halves of the cookie sandwich together with icing. Add colorful "petals" to each side of the flower-pop.

POWDER PUFFS—Shake small cookies in a plastic bag containing powdered sugar. Add a small dollop of icing in each cookie center and top with a colorful candy.

Let each family member choose one special cookie he or she would like to eat, then place six to ten different cookies on each paper plate. Cover the plate with plastic wrap and stick a bow on top. As you nibble your goodies, plan a time to deliver your treats to neighbors, friends, other family members, children's home, or adult care center. Encourage the entire family to go on your "secret kindness mission." End your together-time with a family prayer asking God to show your family ways you can show secret kindness to others.

terrific tip Use this same idea to decorate small cakes, cupcakes, bonbons, and other treats. Or consider purchasing delicious seasonal fruits and decorating fruit baskets to give to others. You might even decorate pretty plates of dried fruits and nuts to give as gifts.

The Poet's Club

Families will discover that praising God is fun.

BIBLE CONCEPT:
We can praise God in our families.

SCRIPTURE BASIS:
Psalms 34:1-3; 108:1-5; 145:1-7

SUPPLIES:
You'll need a Bible, a glue stick, scissors, construction
paper, white paper, and markers.

PREPARATION:
None required.

This activity offers family members the opportunity to express creative praises to God.

Set out the construction paper, scissors, markers, copy paper, and a glue stick. Have family members form pairs. Then instruct each pair to use colored construction paper to create a beautiful picture frame. Cut an inside rectangle from a sheet of construction paper, leaving a two-inch frame around the edge. Then tape a sheet of white copy paper to the center of the frame. Encourage family pairs to decorate their frames using bits of colored paper and markers.

When the frames are finished, invite each family pair to show off its creative efforts. Then set aside the frames and say: **Frames are used to show off beautiful things such as paintings, special stories, or poems. In a moment, we'll make something beautiful to put in our frames. But first, let's see if you can figure out what beautiful thing David gave to God in some of the poems he wrote.** Invite several family members to read aloud Psalms 34:1-3; 108:1-5; and 145:1-7. Then ask:

• **What beautiful thing did David give to God through his poems?**

• **How did David's praises show his love for God?**

• **Why do you think we should praise God?**

65

Say: **Praise poems are a wonderful way to express our love to God, and it's important for our family to praise God together. So let's write praise poems to express our love to God.**

Have each family pair compose a series of verses to praise God. Assure family members that poems don't need to rhyme—they just need to express how they feel about God. Have family members write their poems on the white paper inside their decorative picture frames.

When the poems are complete, read them aloud and encourage everyone to clap after each "praise offering." Then ask:
- **How does praising God bring us closer to God?**
- **How does it bring us closer to those in our family?**
- **What are other ways our family can praise God?**

End your together-time with a prayer thanking God for his love and for your family's ability to praise God together in love. Hang the praise poems throughout the house to remind everyone of the importance of praising God every day.

terrific tip

Look for ways to praise God throughout the week. Learn a simple prayer or song your family can recite or sing at mealtime. Draw pictures of what God has done for various family members during the week, and post them on the refrigerator for everyone to enjoy. Or invite everyone to read his or her favorite psalm to the entire family.

Manna Munchies

Families will recognize that God provides for them.

BIBLE CONCEPT:
God gives us what we need.

SCRIPTURE BASIS:
Exodus 16:13-18, 31; Philippians 4:19-20

SUPPLIES:
You'll need a Bible, a greased cookie sheet, a large mixing bowl, three cups of graham cracker crumbs, plastic sandwich bags, and one cup of marshmallow creme. You'll also need tape.

PREPARATION:
Mix the graham cracker crumbs and marshmallow creme in the mixing bowl. Spread the gooey mixture onto the cookie sheet and chill until firm. Then break apart the "manna," and place chunks of it in plastic sandwich bags. Be sure to prepare at least three bags of "Manna Munchies" for each family member.

This hunt-and-find activity is as delicious as it is devotional—and all ages will eat it up!

Just prior to your together-time, tape the bags of Manna Munchies around the room. Hide some of the bags in more difficult places for older kids and adults to find. Be sure to keep track of how many bags are hidden.

Then gather family members and ask:

● **When is a time you needed something and received it?**

● **How did you feel when you had that need met?**

Say: **Let's read about a time God provided for some hungry people's needs. When you hear what food God gave these people, rub your tummies. When you hear where God put their food, clap your hands two times.** Ask a family member to read aloud Exodus 16:13-18, 31. Then ask:

67

- **What did God provide for the hungry people?**
- **Where did God put their food?**
- **How do you think the hungry people felt when God provided for them?**

Say: **Now let's go on our own manna hunt. Look for bags of pretend manna and see how many you can find!** When all the bags have been collected, gather the family. Divide the bags so everyone has an equal number to nibble on. As everyone enjoys the Manna Munchies, read Philippians 4:19-20, and ask the following questions:

- **How does God provide for our needs every day?**
- **Do you think God knows all our needs? Explain.**
- **Why do you think God provides for us? for our family?**
- **How can we thank God for providing for our needs?**

End your together-time by joining hands, and offering a prayer of thanks for God's love and provision. Encourage each family member to thank God for one thing he has given to him or her or even the family.

terrific tip For a realistic "manna effect," purchase cotton candy and hide tufts around the room. You may wish to put the tufts in plastic sandwich bags to avoid the "stickies"!

Family Prayer Chain

family ♥ goal:

Families will discover that prayer links them to God.

BIBLE CONCEPT:
Prayer joins us to God.

SCRIPTURE BASIS:
Luke 11:9-10

SUPPLIES:
You'll need scissors, tape, and plenty of eleven-by-two-inch
construction paper or copy paper strips.

PREPARATION:
Practice twisting, taping, and cutting the paper strips to create
interlocking links. Use the following instructions and illustrations to
guide you. During your together-time, you'll teach your family how
to cut their own paper chains.

Older kids and parents will love this "tricky" paper-chain prayer devotion.

Hold up a strip of construction paper or copy paper and say:
**Can you make a chain without cutting apart separate strips of
paper?** Hand each person a piece of paper and let them try to
accomplish your challenge. Then demonstrate how to make a paper
chain using the following steps:

Step 1: Hold a paper strip, give it one full twist, and tape the ends
together to make a twisted loop.

Step 2: Carefully poke the tip of the scissors into the center of
the paper strip, and begin cutting lengthwise down the center of the
strip. Continue until you've cut all the way around the loop. There
should be two loops joined like links in a chain!

Turn one end once
and tape

Cut

Hold up the paper chain and ask:

● **In what ways is prayer like a chain with many links? How
is it different?**

● **How does one prayer for our family join us to God? to
each other?**

Read aloud Luke 11:9-10 from the Bible. Then ask:

● **How do asking for and seeking out answers to our needs bring us closer to God?**

● **Why do you think God always opens the door to answer our families' prayers?**

Say: **Prayer is like a chain with many links. Each link strengthens our faith, our trust, and our love to God and to our family. Just like we can join together links from one piece of paper, one prayer can link us to God and each other!**

Have each family member make a paper chain from a strip of paper. Then invite family members to stand in a circle and hold their paper chains. Go around the circle and have each person offer a small prayer of thanks for the family and for family prayer. Then tape the chains into one long chain, and hang it above your dining table. Be sure to offer a prayer of thanksgiving each time the family gathers for mealtime.

terrific tip

If you have very young children, help them make prayer chains by looping strips of colored construction paper around each other and taping them together to make chain links. Challenge young children to add another link each time they pray during the week.

Movers 'n' Shakers

Families will learn that loads are lighter when they're shared.

BIBLE CONCEPT:
God wants us to share our troubles.

SCRIPTURE BASIS:
Romans 12:15

SUPPLIES:
You'll need a Bible.

PREPARATION:
Choose a room you'd like to rearrange. This would be a perfect family devotion for moving day!

Become real "movers 'n' shakers" with this constructive, cooperative family activity—and learn about sharing troublesome loads. Gather your family in the room you'd like to rearrange. Ask:

● **When was a time that you needed help?**
● **How did you feel when you received help?**
● **How can cooperation and helping each other make things easier?**

Say: **Today we're going to see how helping one another really does lighten the loads we carry. Let's pretend we're from the Helping Hands Moving Company, and we're here to move furniture and rearrange this room. So find a moving partner, and let's get moving!**

Cooperatively decide how you'd like the room to be rearranged, then turn your team of movers and shakers loose. Explain that family members can only move an object or item if both partners carry it. Encourage everyone by making comments such as "Wow! This chair is easier to move when my partner helps carry it!" and "I couldn't have done this alone!"

71

When the room is exactly as you want it, gather your movers and ask:

- **What was the hardest part of rearranging the room? What made it easier?**
- **How is carrying heavy troubles like carrying heavy furniture or boxes?**
- **What happens when we share our heavy troubles with someone else?**
- **How can sharing our problems with family members make our problems lighter?**

Ask several volunteers to read aloud Romans 12:15. Then say: **When we share our troubles, they aren't as heavy and troublesome. God wants us to share both the good times and the bad times we may have. When you share your troubles and let the family help, then everyone has a chance to do something nice and show love for you. That's pretty neat, isn't it?**

Then have each family member answer the following questions. Ask:

- **What's one trouble you can share with someone this week?**
- **How can you help carry someone's heavy load this week?**

End your together-time with the following prayer. Cooperatively lift the heaviest piece of furniture in the room when you get to the appropriate place in the prayer, then set it down as you say "amen." Pray: **Dear God, some troubles are just too heavy for us to carry alone. We thank you for sending people to help us lift and carry those troubles.** Lift the piece of furniture. **We know that with your love and each other's help, there is no load too heavy to handle. Amen.**

terrific tip

A simpler version of this activity is to choose a family member to sit in a straight chair, and have each family member try to lift that person and chair by himself or herself. Then have the entire family lift the person and chair a few inches off the ground.

The Terrific Taffy Pull

family ♥ goal:

Families will learn that it's important for them to "stick" together.

BIBLE CONCEPT:
God wants us to love and support each other.

SCRIPTURE BASIS:
Philippians 4:14

SUPPLIES:
You'll need the ingredients and utensils listed in the "Terrific Taffy" recipe below.

PREPARATION:
Soften the butter.

Terrific Taffy

Mix 2 cups white sugar, 1 cup light corn syrup, 1½ teaspoons salt, and 1 cup water in a pot. Stir over low heat until the sugar is completely dissolved.

Turn the heat up to medium-high, and continue cooking and constantly stirring until candy reaches 265 degrees on a candy thermometer (hard-ball stage).

Remove from heat, and stir in 2 tablespoons butter. Pour the "liquid" candy into a buttered 15x10x1-inch pan, and let it cool until it's comfortable to handle.

Butter your hands well, then gather the candy into a ball and pull! Pull and gather, until the taffy is light in color and hard to pull.

Divide the taffy into 4 sections, then stretch each section into 1 long ½-inch-thick strand. Use buttered scissors to cut each strand into bite-sized pieces, then wrap each piece in wax paper.

This great family treat is as fun to make as it is to eat—and it provides a sweet visual of what it means to "stick together."

Place the ingredients on a counter beside the stove. Gather your family in the kitchen and say: **Welcome to the Sweet-Stickies Candy Shop. In this candy kitchen, there isn't one special candy cook. There's a whole family full of 'em! And all the cooks at the Sweet-Stickies Candy Shop stick together and help each other. Today we'll be making a really sticky sweet treat—taffy. And to make this taffy turn out just right, everyone needs to pull together.**

Follow the recipe for Terrific Taffy in the recipe box. Be sure each family member has a turn in the preparation. Young children can stir and mix the sugar and corn syrup as older children measure and pour ingredients.

When the taffy is ready to pull, let it cool slightly on the cookie sheet or clean counter while family members butter their hands generously! Adults should begin the taffy pull because the taffy will probably be too hot for children's hands. As you pull, the taffy will thicken and become more stiff. As the taffy stiffens, let children join in the cooperative pull. Explain that you need lots of hands to stretch the taffy as it cools! Make comments such as "Taffy is so sticky—look how it sticks to our hands and to the pan!" and "Good thing we're pulling together to stretch the taffy before it cools."

When the taffy is difficult to pull, quickly divide your family into crews of Snippers, Wrappers, and Twisters. Have the Snippers cut off bite-sized pieces of taffy and hand them to the Wrappers. Let the Wrappers wrap each piece of taffy in a small piece of wax paper and hand it to the Twisters to twist the ends of the candy papers.

When all the pieces of taffy are snipped, wrapped, and twisted, wash your hands and take a "breather." Ask:
- **What was it like to stick together to help make the taffy?**
- **What would have happened if we hadn't helped each other?**
- **How does sticking together help our family get things done?**
- **In what ways does sticking together show love for each other? support? trust?**

Say: **The Bible tells us that we're to stick together and help each other. In that way, we can accomplish big things. It would have been very hard—if not impossible—to make all this delicious**

taffy alone. But we stuck together and did it! Yea for our family! Lead everyone in a round of lively applause. Then say: **Now let's stick together as we enjoy some sticky treats!**

terrific tip

For smaller families—or for a less involved activity—try making sticky cereal bars. Melt 2 tablespoons butter with a package of small marshmallows. When the marshmallows are melted, stir them into 6 cups crisp rice cereal. Then spread the sticky mixture onto a greased cookie sheet and chill.

FAMILY FESTIVALS

Pleasin' Parties, Festive Foods & Holiday Celebrations

January Jamboree

*Families will learn that each day brings
a new choice to follow God.*

BIBLE CONCEPT:
We choose to follow God because we love him.

SCRIPTURE BASIS:
Joshua 24:15c

SUPPLIES:
You'll need a Bible, coffee filters, scissors,
vanilla ice cream, and chocolate chips.

PREPARATION:
None required.

A wintry day and young children will make this chilly-willy family
activity especially fun.

Set out the coffee filters and scissors. Demonstrate how to fold
the coffee filters into halves, fourths, and eighths; then make small
snips and cuts around all the edges. When the filters are unfolded,
voilà!—instant "snowflakes"! Let young children fold the filters, but
help them with the cutting. Hand the folded filters to the children to
unfold and discover their own snowy designs. Cut three snowflakes
per person, then play the following games.

SNOWFLAKE FOLLOW THE LEADER—Have everyone toss one of the
snowflakes in the air, then imitate the snowflake as it falls to the
ground. See how quickly you can "make it snow." Point out how we
can twist and twirl to follow the snowflakes as they fall.

SNOWFLAKE STEPPINGSTONES—Have one person hold the
snowflakes as other family members hide their eyes. Then have the
snowflake holder lay snowflake "steppingstones" on the floor for others
to follow. You can create as many paths as you want, but have the
snowflake holder stand at the end of one of the paths. When someone

finds the holder, he or she gets to lay the next path to follow.

SNOWFLAKE SNATCH—Place the snowflakes on the floor in a scattered design. Have everyone place one finger on a snowflake. When you say, "Go snow," have everyone find a new snowflake to put his or her finger on. Tell everyone there can be only one person on each snowflake. Then remove a snowflake from play. Continue until someone is finally left without a snowflake. That person must go to the "snow fort" at one side of the room but can cheer for the remaining players. Play until only one person is left touching a snowflake.

When you're through playing, gather everyone in a group and say: **When snowflakes fall to the ground, some of them dance and swirl, twist and twirl in different directions. Other snowflakes seem to follow each other to the ground. But snowflakes don't have a choice about following each other. They just go wherever the wind sends them.** Ask:

- **Do we have a choice about who we follow? Explain.**
- **Who is someone we choose to follow?**
- **Why is it important to choose to follow God every day?**
- **In what ways can we follow God every day?**

Encourage family members to name ways they can follow God, such as reading the Bible, learning God's Word, obeying God, praying, going to church, and learning more about Jesus.

Read aloud Joshua 24:15c. Then say: **Each morning, we have a new choice: whether to follow God or not to follow. But we know that God loves us, so it's a smart choice to follow God in all we do. Choosing to follow God means going where God wants us to go and following the paths he sets out for us. And the great part is—our whole family can choose to follow God at the same time!**

End the activity by inviting everyone to make a chilly treat—
Tracks in the Snow. Scoop vanilla ice cream into bowls, then provide
chocolate chips and have family members make "paths" in their ice
cream. Encourage them to nibble the paths gone by following the
patterns of chocolate chips. As you enjoy your cool snacks, visit
about what choosing to follow God can do for your family.

terrific tip It's often difficult for young children to concretely understand the abstract concept of "following God." To help
them grasp this idea, prepare unsweetened Kool-Aid without
following the directions to add sugar. After tasting the "following fail-
ure," talk about the consequences of not following what we should
and why it's so very important to choose to follow God.

Groundhog Hullabaloo

family ♥ goal:

*Families will learn that God sticks to
them when they stick to him!*

BIBLE CONCEPT:
God is faithful.

SCRIPTURE BASIS:
Psalm 100:5

SUPPLIES:
You'll need a Bible, black construction paper, a flashlight, bananas,
chocolate chips, craft sticks, wax paper, and a bowl or a basket.

PREPARATION:
Cut the following "shadow shapes" from black construction paper: a
flower, a butterfly, a house, an ice-cream cone, and a heart. Cut out
one shape for each family member. If your family is larger than five,
cut out a different shape for each additional person.

This festive family activity is "shadowy" fun—and shines forth the bright love of God's faithfulness.

Hide the shadow shapes around the room. Invite family members to the Groundhog Hullabaloo—ask them to bring their shadows with them.

Welcome family members to the Groundhog Hullabaloo by shining the flashlight on each person and welcoming his or her shadow, too. Then say: **I'm so glad our family is here to share in the shadows and fun of our Groundhog Hullabaloo. What's special about groundhogs?** Let everyone tell their ideas, then explain the tradition: If a groundhog sees its shadow on February 2, there will be six more weeks of winter.

Say: **Today we'll use groundhogs and shadows to learn something very important. But first, we need to find some missing shadows! Go on a shadow hunt and, when you find one, bring it back to the center of the room.** When everyone has a shadow shape, play one or more of the following games.

SHADOW CHARADES—Place the shadow shapes in a basket or a bowl. Let family members take turns secretly choosing a shadow shape, then acting it out. See how long it takes the others to guess the shape.

SHADOW TAG—Scatter the shadow shapes on the floor. Choose one person to be the "Shadow Monster," who will try to tag the other players before they stand on and imitate a shadow shape. If someone is tagged, he or she must become a "shadow" and stand in back of the Shadow Monster with hands on the Shadow Monster's shoulders. Then the two must try to tag others. Play until only one person is not part of the Shadow Monster.

SHADOW SHAPERS—Using the flashlight, take turns making shadowy figures on the wall, ceiling, or floor. Guess the shapes each family member makes.

After playing several games, gather family members and ask:

● **What do you think is special about a shadow?**

● **How does a shadow show its "faithfulness" by staying beside you all the time?**

● **How is God like a loving "shadow shape"?**

Say: **God shows us his faithfulness by staying with us just as a shadow stays with us. God loves us, follows us, and stays connected to us all the time. When we love God, he sticks with us no matter what. Now <u>that's</u> faithfulness! Let's see what the Bible says about God's faithfulness.**

Read aloud Psalm 100:5. Point out how God's faithfulness comes from his great love and that when we are faithful to God, he is faithful to us. Ask:

● **In what ways is God's faithfulness important to our family?**

● **How can our family thank God for his faithfulness?**

Offer a prayer thanking God for his love and faithfulness. Then troop into the kitchen to make Groundhog Goodies. Melt a package of chocolate chips in the microwave or in a double boiler. Have kids peel bananas, cut them in half, and poke clean craft sticks into the bananas. Then dip the banana "groundhogs" in melted chocolate and place them on wax paper in the freezer for thirty minutes. As the Groundhog Goodies harden and freeze, read aloud the poem "My Shadow" by Robert Louis Stevenson (p. 83), or play another game.

As you nibble your tasty treats, talk about ways God has shown his faithfulness to your family. Invite family members to each keep a paper shadow as a reminder that God's faithfulness follows us everywhere we go.

terrific tip Very young children will enjoy matching and playing with sets of paper shadow shapes—and the reinforcement will remind them of God's faithfulness.

MY SHADOW

Robert Louis Stevenson

I have a little shadow that goes in and out with me,
And what can be the use of him is more than I can see.
He is very, very like me from the heels up to the head;
And I see him jump before me, when I jump into my bed.

The funniest thing about him is the way he likes to grow—
Not at all like proper children, which is always very slow;
For he sometimes shoots up taller like an india-rubber ball,
And he sometimes goes so little that there's none of him at all.

He hasn't got a notion of how children ought to play,
And can only make a fool of me in every sort of way.
He stays so close behind me, he's a coward you can see;
I'd think shame to stick to nursie as that shadow sticks to me!

One morning, very early, before the sun was up,
I rose and found the shining dew on every buttercup;
But my lazy little shadow, like an arrant sleepy-head,
Had stayed at home behind me and was fast asleep in bed.

New Creation Celebration

Families will discover that Jesus brings joy through the new life of Easter.

BIBLE CONCEPT:

When we love Jesus, we become joyous new creations.

SCRIPTURE BASIS:

2 Corinthians 5:17

SUPPLIES:

You'll need a Bible, plastic eggs, vinegar, small bowls, food coloring, spoons, crayons, paper towels, dull pennies, a dozen hard-boiled eggs, a basket, a bow, and an Easter card. You'll also need a batch of Surprise Cupcakes made from the recipe included in this activity and photocopies of the "New Creation Celebration" invitation on page 87.

PREPARATION:

Photocopy the "New Creation Celebration" invitation (p. 87). Slip one invitation inside a plastic egg for each family member. Make Surprise Cupcakes using the recipe below. Be sure to prepare one cupcake for each person.

Surprise Cupcakes

Prepare a box of cake mix according to the directions on the package—but don't bake the batter. Fill ice-cream cones half full of cake batter, then add a gumdrop. Continue to fill the cone to one inch from the top. Bake according to directions or until golden brown. Cool and decorate with icing, shredded green coconut, and tiny jelly beans.

This spunky party is a celebration of the newness of spring—and of our hearts when we love Jesus!

Distribute the plastic eggs. Hide the eggs outside of each person's bedroom door for a secret surprise. If someone inquires about what "new" or "different" thing to wear, suggest borrowing something from another family member, making a new paper hat, or wearing a shirt backward.

Be sure the Surprise Cupcakes are prepared. You may wish to decorate a festive party table by covering it with Easter gift wrap and setting the table with colorful paper goods. For an extra touch, fill an Easter basket with fresh flowers and place it in the center of the table. Fresh flowers colorfully accentuate the party theme of "new life."

Gather family members and warmly welcome them to the New Creation Celebration. Say: **I see you all have on something "new." Can you guess what each other's new item is?** Encourage family members to tell their guesses about what "new" item each person is wearing. Have each family member explain what is new and different. Then ask:

● **Does wearing something new or different make you a different person? Why or why not?**

● **If people can't change themselves by what they wear, how do they change?**

● **Who is the only one who can bring us new life so we truly become new creations?**

Say: **Jesus is the only one who helps us become truly new creations. How does he do this? Let's see if the Bible has the answer.** Choose someone to read aloud 2 Corinthians 5:17. Then ask:

● **How do you think we become changed by loving Jesus?**

● **Why is there great joy in being new creations in Christ?**

● **What do you think happens to show we're new creations?**

Invite family members to each take a dull penny and tell ways that we are like dull pennies before we love Jesus. Then drop the pennies in a bowl of vinegar and soak them for several minutes. Play the following games and activities while the pennies soak.

EGG ROLL RELAY—Hand a plastic egg to each person. On "go," challenge players to roll the eggs to the other end of the room in any way they desire such as with their noses or toes or hands. When they reach the opposite end of the room, players must switch eggs with another person and return to their starting places.

EGGHEADS—Hand each person a hard-boiled egg and a crayon. Have family members each draw a happy face on their eggs to show the joy they have in loving Jesus. Encourage everyone to use lots of cheerful crayon colors. Hold the eggs in spoons over bowls, drizzle food coloring over the eggs, and watch as the crayon wax repels the dye. Set the eggs on paper towels to dry.

While the eggs dry, return to the pennies. Hand each person a paper towel and scoop out a penny. Have everyone rub and polish his or her penny until it shines brilliantly. Then ask:

● **How are these shiny pennies like our lives when we love Jesus?**

Say: **When we love Jesus, we become changed like new creations—just as the dull pennies became like new. We know we're new by the joy we feel inside and by the way we're able to love and accept others. There's no greater joy than the joy we have in being new creations in Christ!**

Have family members gather at the party table and help themselves to a Surprise Cupcake. Before enjoying the special treats, offer a prayer thanking God for Jesus' love and for the way we become changed when we love him. Then explain that each Surprise Cupcake has a surprise inside to remind everyone about the way we change inside when we love Jesus. When someone discovers the hidden surprise, he or she is to say, "I'm changed inside—and I love Jesus!"

Let family members keep their shiny pennies to remind them how new and bright their lives are as a result of Jesus' love. Place the decorated eggs in a pretty basket and add a bow and a card on which you've written 2 Corinthians 5:17. Then on Easter morning, secretly place the pretty surprise on an elderly neighbor's doorstep to spread the joy your family feels in loving Christ.

terrific tip

Another way to illustrate how we become changed with Christ's love is to invite children to watch as you prepare another batch of Surprise Cupcakes. Point out that the batter becomes changed from the inside out when you bake it! Share your delicious treats with another family.

You're Invited!
To The
New
Creation
Celebration!

When:

Where:

Bring your plastic egg and wear
something "new" or different!

Report Card Rally

family ♥ goal:

*Families will recognize that God's grace is
more important than grades.*

BIBLE CONCEPT:
God's grace isn't earned.

This unusual family devotion includes a trip to the ice-cream parlor for a cool treat and warm fuzzies for all.

Before gathering family members on the "first report card" night, place a yardstick on a table so only half of it sticks out over the edge. Place several sheets of newspaper over the length of yardstick still on the table. Be sure the newspapers' long edges run along the edge of the table. (See the diagram.)

Call everyone together and hold up the five dollar bill. Say: **I have a great reward for anyone who can whop this yardstick one time and flip the newspapers onto the ground.** This trick looks deceptively simple—yet it can't be done if set up properly. Let each family member have one try at flipping the papers to the floor. Then hold the yardstick up and say: **Well, I guess no one quite measured up. Some of you got close, but you didn't quite do it right. Now what will I do with this great reward?** Pause for a moment, then ask:

● **How do you feel when you aren't perfect at something or can't do it just as someone wants?**

● **How is this activity like receiving grades or merit bonuses at work?**

• **Do you think God measures us by a heavenly yardstick or report card? Explain.**

• **Does God love us no matter how well or poorly we do? Why or why not?**

Say: **God doesn't use a report card to grade us because we would all fail! We couldn't measure up or be perfect enough— only Jesus is perfect. But God still loves us and gives us wonderful blessings and rewards anyway. Why? Because God loves us! How? Because of God's grace. Grace is receiving something wonderful from God when we don't deserve it. Let's read what the Bible says about God's grace.**

Read aloud Ephesians 2:8-10. Then ask:

• **How does it feel to be loved and accepted by God even though we're not perfect?**

• **How is this like our love and acceptance for family members regardless of their grades or merit raises?**

Say: **Love and acceptance go way beyond grades or raises. Love and acceptance, even though we're not perfect, is like God's gift of grace. Now, even though no one could measure up and flip the papers off, let's share the prize by going for ice cream and remembering that God's grace is like this special treat—it's not earned but freely given in love!**

terrific tip Recognize (and remember!) how stressful report card time can be—and realize the difference between grace and grades. As far as report cards go, the most valuable A is for Acceptance!

REPORT CARD	
A	Acceptance
B	Believing in
C	Caring
D	Devotion
F	Family!

Sunrise Picnic Breakfast

family ♥ goal:

Families will discover that they can "rise 'n' shine" for God.

BIBLE CONCEPT:
We can shine God's love to others.

SCRIPTURE BASIS:
Luke 11:33-36

SUPPLIES:
You'll need a Bible, white paper, colored chalk, and a blanket. For your picnic breakfast, bring along orange juice, doughnuts, cold milk, plates, cups, and napkins.

PREPARATION:
None required.

This unusual weekend picnic begins at daybreak—but the good feelings will last all day long!

Plan your breakfast together-time several days in advance. Invite family members to come along for some sunrise fun 'n' frolic—and, of course, food! Choose a nearby park or scenic area and plan out a simple menu consisting of doughnuts, juice, and milk. Let children help pack the picnic breakfast the evening before your event, and be sure to toss in paper plates, napkins, and cups. This would be a great time to use up any "odd" party ware left over from birthdays or other celebrations.

Remind family members to set their alarms for twenty minutes before daybreak—and tell them that a friendly "wake-up service" is also available! Also remind family members to wear sweaters or jackets so they can greet the sunrise without shivers!

When you reach the park, spread out the blanket and take a few moments to be completely still. Look around at the beauty too many people miss in the pursuit of an extra few minutes of sleep. Hand out paper and colored chalk, and encourage everyone to capture the colors of the sunrise on paper.

As you quietly work, whisper: **Isn't the beginning of a new day beautiful? God gives such beauty in the sunrise, but often we miss this special moment—even though it's here for us every day. How do you feel knowing that in a moment the sun will pop up bright and beautiful?** Allow family members a chance to tell their thoughts and feelings.

When the sun actually hops over the horizon, ask:

- **What do you think makes the sun so wonderful?**
- **How does its light and warmth help us? help the world?**
- **How is the bright sunshine like each of us when we love God?**

Say: **We have a warmth and brightness that can only come from loving God. And everyone in our family has that brilliant warmth!** Read aloud Luke 11:33-36. Then ask:

- **What is special about the warmth we receive from God's love?**
- **Why does God want us to spread his love and brightness?**
- **How can we share our brightness and warmth with others?**

Encourage family members to name ways, such as being kind to others, helping people who need our help, sharing God's Word with others, and praying.

Share the beautiful sunrise pictures everyone drew, then offer a sunrise prayer thanking God for the bright love in your lives and for opportunities to share that brilliance with others who may not know God or Jesus. Then enjoy your delicious picnic breakfast as you visit about God's love and how you can shine that love all around the world.

Hang the gallery of daybreak delights around the house when you return from your trip. That way you'll remember the beauty of God's sunrise even on the days you decide to sleep in!

terrific tip For a more memorable time, consider going to a park and actually cooking breakfast outside. Fry some scrambled eggs and bacon, and you'll have a together-time more memorable than any sensational sunrise!

Teddy Bear Picnic

family ♥ goal:

Families will discover that love is meant to be shared.

BIBLE CONCEPT:
God wants us to share our love.

SCRIPTURE BASIS:
John 15:12-13

SUPPLIES:
You'll need teddy bears or other stuffed animals, a picnic lunch, a soft blanket, and photocopies of the "Teddy Bear" pattern on page 94.

PREPARATION:
Prepare a simple picnic lunch such as peanut butter and honey sandwiches, chips, teddy bear shaped cookies, and juice. If you have a teddy bear shaped cookie cutter, use it to cut the sandwiches into fun shapes. Make five photocopies of the "Teddy Bear" pattern (p. 94). Use brown construction paper for the photocopies. Cut out the patterns.

Very young children will adore this lively picnic with their best friends—parents and teddy bears!

Invite your family to a Teddy Bear Picnic. Let your children choose their favorite teddy bears or stuffed animals to attend as their guests. Parents can choose a furry friend from their child's "stuffed zoo" to take along for themselves.

Select a pleasant park for your picnic. Take along the paper teddy bears, the picnic lunch, a soft blanket, and your stuffed friends. As you travel to your destination, sing fun children's songs such as "The Teddy Bears' Picnic," "Winnie the Pooh," or "The Bear Went Over the Mountain."

When you arrive, spread out the blanket and set down the picnic basket or bag. Say: **What a nice day for a picnic! And its especially nice because we're with the ones we love—our family and our very special friends. It's great fun to share our love and the good times we have, isn't it? Before we eat, let's play some fun games with the ones we love!** Play one or more of the following games using the paper teddy bears and stuffed animals.

TEDDY BEAR ROUNDUP—Choose one person to hide the paper teddy bears around the area. You may need to secure them with a small stone or twig. Then have everyone else hunt the teddies. When all the bears are rounded up, choose someone else to hide them again.

TEDDY RHYME TIME—Say the following rhyme using the paper teddy bears or your own fingers as "teddies."

> Five little teddy bears—furry balls of fun. (*Squat down.*)
> One bounced away, then four were in the sun. (*Bounce up and down.*)
> Four little teddy bears—furry balls of fun. (*Squat down.*)
> One bounced away, then three were in the sun. (*Bounce up and down.*)
> Three little teddy bears...
> Two little teddy bears...
> One little teddy bear...

TEDDY BEAR TAG—Hold your teddies and hop to tag an opponent's bear. When a bear is tagged, go to the "honey pot" (blanket) in the center of your playing area. Continue until all the bears (and players) are in the honey pot.

TEDDY BEAR, WHAT DO I SEE?—Play this quiet color game just before lunch. Take turns repeating and filling in the blank of the following rhyme, with everyone else guessing what is being observed.

> Teddy Bear, Teddy Bear,
> What do I see?
> I see something (color of an object)
> Looking at me!

As you and your teddies enjoy the delicious picnic, discuss the following questions:

- Why is it important to share our love with others?
- What happens when love spreads to many, many people?
- Who loves us sooo much that he shares his love with us all the time?

Say: **God loves us more than anything, and he is always sharing his love with us. God knows that when we feel his love, we'll want to share it with someone else. Then that person feels loved and wants to share it. And the love goes on and on! Loving our teddy bears and other stuffed friends helps us learn to be loving to people.**

- **How can we share our love with others? with our family?**

End your picnic time by having the teddies "help" clean up the picnic area—and the park area. Then troop back home singing "Teddy Bear's Picnic" or "Jesus Loves Me."

Consider taking along the wonderful children's book *Velveteen Rabbit* by Margery Williams. This special love story about a furry stuffed friend and a child is a favorite with children—and adults!

**TEDDY
BEAR**

It's in the Stars!

Families will learn that God's blessings are
as numerous as the stars in the sky.

BIBLE CONCEPT:
God's blessings for us are countless.

SCRIPTURE BASIS:
2 Corinthians 9:10-11

SUPPLIES:
You'll need a Bible, star stickers, cardboard tubes, black construction paper, straight pins, crayons, and tape. You'll also want a flashlight and a simple star constellation chart so you can identify several major constellations.

PREPARATION:
Cut out one three-inch black construction paper circle for each person. Be sure you have a cardboard tube for each person. Bathroom tissue tubes or paper towel tubes cut in half work well for this activity.

This nighttime family devotion will have your family seeing stars—and counting God's blessings in their lives.

Choose a dark area away from city lights to visit on a starry summer night. Look toward the heavens and have family members point out the constellations they recognize. Use the star chart and flashlight to identify constellations and stars such as the Big and Little Dippers; Cygnus the Swan; the Gemini Twins; Polaris, the North Star; and Cassiopeia, the Queen (or Lady in Chair). Encourage everyone to keep his or her eyes peeled for shooting stars and meteors. Challenge family members to count the stars, then finish the sentence, "There are as many stars as..."

As you gaze heavenward, say: **The Bible tells us about a time God told Abraham to look up at the stars. God promised**

95

Abraham that he would have as many descendants or family members as there are stars in the sky. To Abraham, descendants were the most precious of God's blessings, and he was amazed God would give him blessings as countless as the stars! **How do you think Abraham felt when he looked at the stars?** Pause for responses. Then ask:

● **Why do you think God compared his blessings to the stars in the sky?**

● **Why is it impossible to count the blessings we receive from God?**

Read aloud 2 Corinthians 9:10-11. Say: **God blesses us all the time in ways we may not even be aware of. God's blessings surround us every day in countless ways.** Ask:

● **In what ways has God blessed you? our family?**

● **What can we do with all the blessings God gives us?**

● **How can we thank God for the countless blessings he gives us?**

When you return home, make Starry Skyscopes by taping black construction paper circles over one end of each cardboard tube. Use the straight pins to poke holes in the paper circles. Decorate the Skyscopes using star stickers and crayons. Then aim the Starry Skyscopes toward a lamp and peek through them. What do you see? Stars! Stars to remind everyone of God's blessings and the beauty of each blessing he gives.

terrific tip
If you live near a planetarium, plan to visit it before your trip to look at the starry sky. Or visit the library and gather colorfully illustrated books about stars and planets to enjoy as a family. You may even be able to find glow-in-the-dark star stickers to attach to your child's ceiling. What a perfect, peaceful reminder of God's blessings—every night!

First Day of School Celebration

Families will learn that God is with
them wherever they go.

BIBLE CONCEPT:
God is always with us.

SCRIPTURE BASIS:
Joshua 1:9

SUPPLIES:
You'll need a Bible, iced cake, candy sprinkles, ribbon, and party plates, cups, and napkins. You'll also need a selection of party favors such as cute erasers, fancy new pencils, note pads, crayons, and brightly colored rulers.

PREPARATION:
Purchase or prepare an iced cake. Sprinkle candy decorations on top, then gently stick new pencils on or around the cake for colorful party favors.

This great mini-party has the element of surprise—keep the plans secret until your delighted kids waltz in after their first day of school. (If your schedule doesn't permit you to meet your kids when they come home that day, plan the party for later that evening—but make sure your preparations are kept secret!)

While the children are at school, prepare or purchase an iced but undecorated cake. Set the table in a festive fashion using colorful party cups, napkins, and plates. This is a good time to use up any leftover party ware or odd plates and napkins. If you have a couple of balloons (even if they're from the local savings and loan!), blow them up and tape them to the table or chairs. Place the party cake in the center of the table. Wrap ribbons around any party favors you've collected. Place the favors on each party plate. Now wait excitedly for your kids to arrive for their surprise "homecoming."

When your delighted children are gathered around the party table, say: **I'm so glad you're home—and this party is just for YOU! C'mon and sit down, have some cake, and tell me all about your exciting day!** Encourage your kids to share all the fun details of their first day at school—where their lockers are, who they sat with at lunch, who their teachers are, and what classes they have.

Say: **I had a good day, too, but the best part was when I saw you. My thoughts were in school with you all day long, even though I couldn't be there in person. But did you know someone who loves you was with you all day? God was in school with you on your first day—and he will be with you in school every day. That's because God is with us wherever we go. In fact, God says in the Bible, "I will be with you wherever you go."** Read aloud Joshua 1:9. Then say: **It makes me feel good to know that when I can't be there with you, God is! Now, tell me what the best part of your school day was!**

Let kids share more about their first day of school and enjoy their welcome-home party treats and festive favors.

terrific tip

If you have sparklers, place one in the center of the cake, and light it as soon as your kids walk through the door. What a special "You're worth it!" surprise!

Pickle Party

family ♥ goal:

*Families will discover that having fun together
draws families nearer.*

BIBLE CONCEPT:
God wants us to be lighthearted.

SCRIPTURE BASIS:
Psalm 149:1-5

SUPPLIES:
You'll need a Bible, one jar of sweet pickles and one of dill pickles, three small cucumbers, green balloons, green construction paper, green crepe paper, two paper sacks or baskets, markers, and tape. You'll also want party refreshments including cucumbers, fresh vegetables, cucumber salad dressing, crisp crackers, and apple juice.

PREPARATION:
Cut the green construction paper into pickle shapes such as gherkins or dill chips. Cut out at least ten of each shape.

This perky party is sure to make everyone pleased—and puckered!

On the day of your planned party, hand each person a paper pickle and invite him or her to a zany family Pickle Party. Tell everyone to bring the paper pickle to the party.

Set out the party items, foods, and jars of pickles. Gather the family and say: **Welcome to our Pickle Party! Are you ready for some puckering-good times and pickle-tickle laughs? Then let's all pitch in and decorate our party room.** Have everyone help twist and tape green crepe paper streamers across the room and blow up and tie off green balloons. Tape some of the balloons to the streamers, but set several aside for later.

When the room is decorated, play one or more of the following games and activities.

PETER PIPER RELAY—Place the paper pickles in the center of the room and the paper sacks or baskets at the opposite end. Form two teams and assign each team a bag. Explain that the object of this game is to see how many pickles each group can collect in its bag. Team members must take turns walking heel-to-toe to collect a paper pickle and then deposit it in the group's bag. Then the player is to hop back to the team so the next team member can go. Continue until all the paper pickles are in the bags. All the time they are playing, team members must recite the "Peter Piper" tongue twister. Count the pickles at the end of the relay and have the winning group members each eat a pickle of their choice.

PICKLE JUGGLING—Be sure everyone knows that pickles are made from cucumbers. Then have family members stand in a circle. Begin by tossing one cucumber back and forth from one person to another until everyone has been tossed the cucumber. Tell players to toss the cucumber to the same person each time to create a pattern. When a pattern is established, add a second cucumber—then a third. See how long you can "juggle pickles" until one is dropped. Then begin again, but toss to new players. For extra fun, speed up the tossing!

PICKLE PEOPLE—Hand each person a green balloon "pickle" and a marker. Invite family members to draw faces on their inflatable pickles, then give their pickle-people names such as Dill-bert, Q. Cumber, or Gertrude Gherkin. Have everyone introduce his or her pickle-person by name, then line up the pickles. While everyone else covers his or her eyes, have one person remove a pickle. See who can guess which pickle-person is missing.

PICKLE JAR SLALOM—Set the jars of pickles in a staggered line down the center of the room. Be sure there's two feet of space between each jar. Stand at one end of the room with your balloon "pickles." Let one person choose the way family members will travel through the pickle jar slalom course, such as bouncing the balloon pickles, holding the balloon pickles between their knees or under their chins, or scooting the balloon pickles on the floor with their feet. On "go," each player must travel in and out between the pickle jars from one end of the room to the other and back again. Continue until everyone has had a chance to invent a way to travel the slalom course.

When you're ready for a rest, serve refreshments. Dip cucumber slices in bowls of cucumber salad dressing. Nibble pickles and crisp crackers with the raw vegetables. As you unwind, ask:

● **How does having a good time bring us closer together?**

● **Why do you think God smiles when families have good fun?**

Say: **God enjoys our good times as much as we do. That's because God is part of our family, too! Let's read what God says about having a good time and being happy.** Read aloud Psalm 149:1-5. Then ask:

● **How are sharing joy with our family and with other people who love God alike?**

● **How does loving God make for more joy in our family?**

● **What are other fun things you'd like to do with our family?**

Form a circle and say: **Let's end with a "pickle prayer." We'll pass this jar of pickles around the circle. When it comes to you, thank God for one happy memory you have of the family fun we've shared today or any other time.** Continue until each family has had a turn to share, then say "amen."

terrific tip

For extra taste-treat fun and excitement, purchase unusual pickled foods such as pickled watermelon rind, pickled peppers, or pickled pears. Explain to younger children that pickles don't grow on trees or vines but are actually other foods with special spices added.

Pumpkin Party

Families will discover that God gives abundant blessings.

BIBLE CONCEPT:
God blesses our family abundantly.

SCRIPTURE BASIS:
2 Corinthians 9:10-11

SUPPLIES:
You'll need a Bible, newspapers, pumpkins to carve, safety knives, markers, a cookie sheet, large spoons, and a bowl of salt water.

PREPARATION:
None required.

This fall harvest activity will have family members smiling as broadly as their pumpkin counterparts.

Gather your family and ask:

● **What time of year is this? What happens in the fall?**

● **Why do you think farmers are especially happy in the fall?**

Say: **Autumn is a time when all the hard work of planting seeds, growing crops, and weeding gardens is finished. When all that hard work is done, there are loads of delicious fruits, vegetables, and grains to eat. This is harvest time, and God richly gives to us during harvest. What are your favorite fruits and vegetables?** Let everyone share his or her choices. Then say: **God's gifts to us are called blessings, and God richly blesses those whom he loves. Let's see what the Bible tells us about God's blessings.**

Read aloud 2 Corinthians 9:10-11. Then ask:

● **In what ways has God blessed our family?**

● **How does it feel to receive God's blessings?**

Say: **Think of all the things God gives our family.** Pause. **Now think of how happy we are when God blesses us! Let's make pumpkin faces to show how we look when we feel the joy of God's abundant blessings!**

Spread newspapers on a tile, basement, porch, or garage floor.

Have family members pair up so young children are working with an adult. Give each pair a pumpkin, then encourage partners to draw a happy face on their pumpkin. Carve the tops or the "hats" from each pumpkin and scoop out the seeds. Place the seeds (minus the goo!) into a bowl of salt water to soak. When all the seeds have been collected, spread them on a cookie sheet and slowly roast them at 325 degrees until they're golden brown.

As the seeds roast, continue making your "pleased pumpkin" faces. Young children can direct adults as to "where and how" to carve their creations. As you work, talk about the reasons God blesses those he loves and how we can thank God for his gifts through prayer, helping others, and reading the Bible.

When all the pumpkins are carved, invite family members to show off their handiwork. Then line up your pleased pumpkins along your front walk or porch for everyone in the neighborhood to enjoy.

When the pumpkin seeds are done, remove them from the oven and sprinkle on a bit of salt. After the seeds cool, enjoy crunching and munching as you visit about the abundance of the harvest and what other foods are being picked and packed for us to eat.

terrific tip

Take your children on a trip to a pumpkin patch to "harvest" their own pumpkins. If children are very young, limit pumpkin size to ones they can carry. Then have children paint faces on their pumpkins instead of carving them.

Super Slumber Party

Families will learn that God watches
over them all the time.

BIBLE CONCEPT:
God never slumbers or sleeps.

SCRIPTURE BASIS:
Psalm 121:1-8

SUPPLIES:
You'll need a Bible, pillows, blankets or sleeping bags, flashlights (or a candle and matches), pencils, and photocopies of "A Bedtime Story" and "A Bedtime Poem" on page 110. You'll also want to keep on hand simple party refreshments such as chips, dip, and fruit juice served in party cups.

PREPARATION:
Make one photocopy each of "A Bedtime Story" and "A Bedtime Poem" (p. 110) for every two family members. Cut the stories apart.

Kids and grown-ups alike will enjoy this snoozy sleep-over.

Invite family members to gather for an evening of entertainment and a night of snoozing. Have them bring pillows, sleeping bags or blankets, a favorite book or game—and a smile. Encourage everyone to claim a comfy spot and set up "camp." Then have family members get into pairs or trios. Pair nonreaders with readers.

Give each pair or trio the "Bedtime Story" handout and a pencil. (Set the "Bedtime Poem" handout aside.) Challenge partners to come up with the wildest bedtime story possible by filling in the blanks. Then read aloud your crazy bedtime stories and enjoy some good ol' fashioned belly laughs. Clap after each clever narrative performance. Then hand out "A Bedtime Poem," and repeat the process, clapping after each reading.

Turn out the lights as you turn on the flashlights or light the candle. Ask:

● **When's a time you were afraid of the dark or afraid to go to sleep?** Encourage everyone to share his or her experiences.

● **What helps when you're afraid at night—or any time?**

Say: **Do you know that there's someone who's always on guard, protecting us through every day and night? There's someone who never sleeps, who never slumbers. Listen as I read from the Bible. When you know who never sleeps, put your hand on your head.** Read aloud Psalm 121:1-8. Then ask:

● **Who never slumbers or sleeps?**

● **Why do you think God stays awake?**

● **How does knowing that God watches over our family all day and all night make you feel?**

Then use the flashlights to play a game. Shine a light on a family member and say: **God watches over you, in the day and nighttime, too.** Then pass the flashlight to that person, and let him or her shine the light and repeat the rhyme. Continue until each family member has had a turn to shine the light.

Say: **It makes me feel good to know that I never have to be afraid at night. I know that God is with me all the time. And he is with our family all the time, too. Let's say a bedtime prayer thanking God for never leaving us alone.** Offer a prayer of thanks, then serve the party refreshments. Before you settle down for a good night's sleep, read a storybook your children may have brought.

terrific tip

If parents prefer not to go to sleep so early, have them quietly read or watch a movie as their children sleep. Kids will experience the security of knowing someone is watching over them as they slumber and sleep.

Advent Event

Families will discover that God keeps his promises.

BIBLE CONCEPT:
God keeps his promises.

SCRIPTURE BASIS:
2 Corinthians 1:20-22

SUPPLIES:
You'll need a Bible, a straw wreath, tacky craft glue, a paper plate lined with aluminum foil, green and red construction paper, three purple candles, one pink or rose candle, and one chunky white pillar candle. You'll also need florist clay, available at craft or florist shops.

PREPARATION:
None required.

Help your family feel the holiday promises this season holds—and the everlasting love of God's greatest promise to us.

Plan this activity toward the end of November so you have the full Advent season for the family activities, which will stretch out over the course of several weeks.

During the week prior to the fourth Sunday before Christmas, set out the craft materials and gather family members. Ask:

● **What's a promise?**

● **What's the best promise someone made and kept to you?**

● **How is Christmas a season of special promises and gifts?**

Say: **A promise is an assurance or vow we give to someone. Promises are made in great faith and require lots of trust that they will be kept. It's not good to break promises, yet we've all felt the sting of a broken promise at one time or another. Did you know there's someone who never ever breaks his promises? Listen as we read from the Bible. When you know who never breaks his promises, put your hand on your heart.**

Invite someone to read aloud 2 Corinthians 1:20-22. When everyone's hand is on his or her heart, say: **Your hands are on your** hearts to show how much love it takes to keep promises. And since God's love is perfect, so are his promises. Now let's read from the Bible once more to find out what God's most special promise was!

Read aloud 2 Corinthians 1:20-22 once more, then ask:

● **Who was God's most special promise?**

● **How do you think the people felt when God made this promise?**

● **How do you think it felt to wait for God to keep this special promise?**

Say: **God promised us the birth of his only Son—Jesus. But it must have been hard to wait for that promise to be kept! We celebrate Christmas to remember Christ's birthday. But we celebrate Advent to remember how God promised us that Jesus would come. Advent is the four weeks leading up to Christmas, and it's during this time that we remember and celebrate the fact that God keeps his promises. It's a time of getting ready for God's promise of Jesus. Today let's get ready for Christmas by making a family Advent wreath to help us celebrate this special season.**

Have family members tear out green construction paper "holly" leaves" and red construction paper "berries." Glue the leaves to the straw wreath with tacky craft glue. Explain that the green leaves represent evergreens, which symbolize the eternal life that is ours through Jesus. Overlap the leaves so the wreath is well-covered; then glue on the red paper berries, which represent the blood Jesus shed for our sins. As you work together, talk about special promises God has made, such as the promise from the story of Noah and the ark or how God promises eternal life through Jesus. Encourage family members to list the promises God has made and kept for your family, such as God's promise of care and protection, love and a warm place to live, and so on.

Place the wreath on the paper plate lined with aluminum foil. Then divide the florist clay into four equal lumps. Stick the lumps opposite each other on the paper plate, inside the wreath. Push three purple candles and one pink candle into the lumps of clay to secure the candles. Set the white pillar candle in the center of the wreath. Mention that the four purple and pink candles stand for the four weeks of Advent and the white candle in the center represents the purity of Jesus.

When the Advent wreath is finished, explain to your family the significance of each candle and color. Then, beginning on the first Sunday after November 26, light each candle, and read the prayer that accompanies it on the "Advent Prayers" box (p. 109).

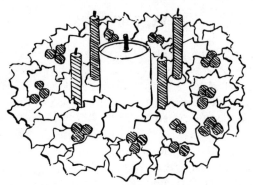

Place the finished Advent wreath on your dining table, and light the candles on the appropriate days. Before lighting a new candle, be sure the previous ones are lit as well. Then offer a family prayer of thanksgiving for God's promises and for his greatest promise of all—Jesus! You may wish to have a different family member pray during each candle-lighting.

For extra fun, serve a tasty dessert that "coordinates" with the candle being lit. For example, serve frozen grapes sprinkled with granulated sugar with the lighting of the first candle, raspberry sherbet or sorbet with the second candle, and plum pudding with the third candle. Serve strawberry shortcake for the lighting of the pink candle, and angel food cake with the white Christ Candle.

terrific tip

On the following weeks, look for ways to celebrate God's promise of Jesus' birth, such as wrapping special "promises" for needy people, making mangers from matchboxes and straw or toothpicks, or giving family members promises of household help—then keeping the promises!

ADVENT PRAYERS

PURPLE CANDLE 1—The candle of HOPE. Light this candle the first Sunday of Advent. Pray: **Dear God, as we light this candle we anticipate the arrival of Jesus in the world and in our hearts, and we faithfully await his return to this world. Thank You, God, for the hope we have in Jesus. Amen.**

PURPLE CANDLE 2—The candle of PEACE. Light this candle the second Sunday of Advent. Pray: **Dear God, we light this second candle of Advent to announce the impending birth of Jesus, our Savior. We know that our peace, and the hope and peace of all who love him, are in Jesus. Amen.**

PINK CANDLE—The candle of JOY. (The pink candle is often referred to as the Rose Candle. Some churches light this candle on the fourth Sunday of Advent. If you choose to do this, simply switch this Sunday with the following.) Light this candle the third Sunday of Advent. Pray: **Dear God, we light this candle to remind us that Jesus is the fulfillment of all your promises and that through Jesus we find everlasting joy. Amen.**

PURPLE CANDLE 3—The candle of LOVE. Light this candle on the fourth Sunday of Advent. Pray: **Dear God, we light this candle to remind us of your great love for us in sending your only Son to be our Savior and Redeemer. Thank you, God, for your wondrous gift of eternal love. Amen.**

WHITE CANDLE—This candle is called the Christ Candle, and stands for Jesus' purity. Light this candle on Christmas Eve or Christmas Day. Pray: **Dear God, we light this white candle to remind us of the greatest gift of your redeeming love, who is Jesus Christ. Thank you, God, for the love and salvation that are ours in your precious Son. Amen.**

A Bedtime Story

Bedtime is my favorite time of all. When I get ready for

bed, I brush my _____ with toothpaste. Toothpaste is
$\qquad$ (noun)

_____ and tastes like _____. Then I wash my
(adjective)   (a food)

_____ with _____ soap. Soap smells like _____
(noun)   (adjective)   (plural noun)

but cleans my face nicely. Then I jump into bed and lay my

_____ on my _____. It's so _____! I pull my
(noun)   (noun)   (adjective)

_____ over me to keep warm, then I say my prayers.
(plural noun)

Good night!

A Bedtime Poem

A _____ sleeps in a nest in a tree,
(noun)

A big scaly _____ snores in the sea.
(noun)

A _____ snake snoozes in _____ wavy weeds,
(adjective)   (color)

A feathery _____ takes a nap in the reeds.
(noun)

Everyone sleeps in some _____ spot.
(adjective)

I sleep in a _____ or a hammock or cot.
(noun)

But there is someone who never sleepily nods—

Who never slumbers? The answer is...God!

Scripture Index

Group Publishing, Inc.
Attention: Books & Curriculum
P.O. Box 481
Loveland, CO 80539
Fax: (970) 669-1994

Evaluation for *AFFORDABLE FAMILY FUN*

Please help Group Publishing, Inc., continue to provide innovative and useful resources for ministry. Please take a moment to fill out this evaluation and mail or fax it to us. Thanks!

1. As a whole, this book has been (circle one)

not very helpful   very helpful

1   2   3   4   5   6   7   8   9   10

2. The best things about this book:

3. Ways this book could be improved:

4. Things I will change because of this book:

5. Other books I'd like to see Group publish in the future:

6. Would you be interested in field-testing future Group products and giving us your feedback? If so, please fill in the information below:

Name _____

Street Address _____

City_____ State _____ Zip _____

Phone Number _____ Date_____